Part 11 • Scope and Application

**The Code of Federal Regulations
Title 21 – Food and Drugs**

Part 11
ELECTRONIC RECORDS;
ELECTRONIC SIGNATURES

GUIDANCE FOR INDUSTRY
PART 11
SCOPE AND APPLICATION
August 2003

AF000056

Printed by GMP Publications, Inc.
Tel: 866-544-9007 or 856-810-7331
Fax: 866-544-9002
http://www.gmppublications.com
sales@gmppublications.com

PART 11--ELECTRONIC RECORDS; ELECTRONIC SIGNATURES

Subpart A--General Provisions

§11.1　　　Scope
§11.2　　　Implementation
§11.3　　　Definitions

Subpart B--Electronic Records

§11.10　　Controls for closed systems
§11.30　　Controls for open systems
§11.50　　Signature manifestations
§11.70　　Signature/record linking

Subpart C--Electronic Signatures

§11.100　　General requirements
§11.200　　Electronic signature components and controls
§11.300　　Controls for identification codes/passwords

Authority: 21 U.S.C. 321-393; 42 U.S.C. 262.

Source: 62 FR 13464, Mar. 20, 1997, unless otherwise noted.

US/EU GMPs
ICH Guideline

Part 11
ELECTRONIC RECORDS; ELECTRONIC SIGNATURES

Parts 210 & 211
cGMP IN MANUFACTURING, PROCESSING, PACKING, OR HOLDING OF DRUGS AND FINISHED PHARMACEUTICALS

Part 820
QUALITY SYSTEM REGULATION

INTRODUCTION
CHAPTER 1 • PHARMACEUTICAL QUALITY SYSTEM
CHAPTER 2 • PERSONNEL
CHAPTER 3 • PREMISES AND EQUIPMENT
CHAPTER 4 • DOCUMENTATION
CHAPTER 5 • PRODUCTION
CHAPTER 6 • QUALITY CONTROL
CHAPTER 7 • CONTRACT MANUFACTURE AND ANALYSIS
CHAPTER 8 • COMPLAINTS AND PRODUCT RECALLS
CHAPTER 9 • SELF INSPECTION
GLOSSARY

ICH Q7
GMPs FOR ACTIVE PHARMACEUTICAL INGREDIENTS

Printed by GMP Publications, Inc.
Tel: 866-544-9007 or 856-810-7331
Fax: 866-544-9002
http://www.gmppublications.com
sales@gmppublications.com

FDA.COM
On-Line Information Portal
& Discussion Groups

FDA.COM is an internet communications site dedicated to supporting the regulated industry by providing a free on-line portal, focusing on the mutual sharing of professional and Government Food, Drug and Regulated information through interactive topic specific discussion groups, online databases and instant access.

FDA.COM is the 'next step', taking industry professionals and visitors beyond The Food and Drug Administration Department. Where the Food and Drug Administration provides the regulations that creates the Laws that Pharmaceuticals, Biotechnology and other Regulated Industry must abide to, they lack in providing a forum of discussing or guiding the industry as to the 'How' and 'Why' to comply.

Every day, thousands of industry professionals come to FDA.COM to find guidance. FDA.COM delivers immediate streamlined quality information to the industry professionals by industry leaders.

Discussion Groups and Open Forums
Food & Drug Administration Links
GMP, GLP, GCP Assistance
Seminars and Conference Listings
Regulatory Guidance
Databases Archives
Guidance Documents Repository
Global Market Place
Classified
e-Newsletters
Templates and Forms Repository
Career Centers and Resume Banks
Advertising Assistance and Promotions

Become a FDA.COM Sponsor today. Sponsors are Industry Leaders, Vendors, Contractors or Professional Service firms, who would field technical and compliance issues by the industry. Sponsors currently enjoy the exclusivity of sponsoring their field or technology sector, and by assisting the industry, enables those Sponsors to stand out as the authoritarian leaders of their specific industry. And at the same time allowing industry leaders to promote their services and products!

Marketing your products or services? With over 2,000,000 visitors a month, FDA.COM is the world's premier global regulatory information resource.

FDA.COM
866-544-9001
Fax 866-544-9002
info@fda.com

Subpart A--General Provisions
§11.1 Scope.

(a) The regulations in this part set forth the criteria under which the agency considers electronic records, electronic signatures, and handwritten signatures executed to electronic records to be trustworthy, reliable, and generally equivalent to paper records and handwritten signatures executed on paper.

(b) This part applies to records in electronic form that are created, modified, maintained, archived, retrieved, or transmitted, under any records requirements set forth in agency regulations. This part also applies to electronic records submitted to the agency under requirements of the Federal Food, Drug, and Cosmetic Act and the Public Health Service Act, even if such records are not specifically identified in agency regulations. However, this part does not apply to paper records that are, or have been, transmitted by electronic means.

(c) Where electronic signatures and their associated electronic records meet the requirements of this part, the agency will consider the electronic signatures to be equivalent to full handwritten signatures, initials, and other general signings as required by agency regulations, unless specifically excepted by regulation(s) effective on or after August 20, 1997.

(d) Electronic records that meet the requirements of this part may be used in lieu of paper records, in accordance with §11.2, unless paper records are specifically required.

(e) Computer systems (including hardware and software), controls, and attendant documentation maintained under this part shall be readily available for, and subject to, FDA inspection.

(f) This part does not apply to records required to be established or maintained by §§1.326 through 1.368 of this chapter. Records that satisfy the requirements of part I, subpart J of this chapter, but that also are required under other applicable statutory provisions or regulations, remain subject to this part.

(g) This part does not apply to electronic signatures obtained under §101.11(d) of this chapter.

(h) This part does not apply to electronic signatures obtained under §101.8(d) of this chapter.

(i) This part does not apply to records required to be established or maintained by part 117 of this chapter. Records that satisfy the requirements of part 117 of this chapter, but that also are required under other applicable statutory provisions or regulations, remain subject to this part.

(j) This part does not apply to records required to be established or maintained by part 507 of this chapter. Records that satisfy the requirements of part 507 of this chapter, but that also are required under other applicable statutory provisions or regulations, remain subject to this part.

(k) This part does not apply to records required to be established or maintained by part 112 of this chapter. Records that satisfy the requirements of part 112 of this chapter, but that also are required under other applicable statutory provisions or regulations, remain subject to this part.

(l) This part does not apply to records required to be established or maintained by subpart L of part 1 of this chapter. Records that satisfy the requirements of subpart L of part 1 of this chapter, but that also are required under other applicable statutory provisions or regulations, remain subject to this part.

(m) This part does not apply to records required to be established or maintained by subpart M of part 1 of this chapter. Records that satisfy the requirements of subpart M of part 1 of this chapter, but that also are required under other applicable statutory provisions or regulations, remain subject to this part.

(n) This part does not apply to records required to be established or maintained by subpart O of part 1 of this chapter. Records that satisfy the requirements of subpart O of part 1 of this chapter, but that also are required under other applicable statutory provisions or regulations, remain subject to this part.

(o) This part does not apply to records required to be established or maintained by part 121 of this chapter. Records that satisfy the requirements of part 121 of this chapter, but that also are required under other applicable statutory provisions or regulations, remain subject to this part.

[62 FR 13464, Mar. 20, 1997, as amended at 69 FR 71655, Dec. 9, 2004; 79 FR 71253, Dec. 1, 2014; 80 FR 71253, June 19, 2015; 80 FR 56144, 56336, Sept. 17, 2015; 80 FR 74352, 74547, 74667, Nov. 27, 2015; 81 FR 20170, Apr. 6, 2016; 81 FR 34218, May 27, 2016]

§11.2 Implementation.

(a) For records required to be maintained but not submitted to the agency, persons may use electronic records in lieu of paper records or electronic signatures in lieu of traditional signatures, in whole or in part, provided that the requirements of this part are met.

(b) For records submitted to the agency, persons may use electronic records in lieu of paper records or electronic signatures in lieu of traditional signatures, in whole or in part, provided that:

(1) The requirements of this part are met; and

(2) The document or parts of a document to be submitted have been identified in public docket No. 92S-0251 as being the type of submission the agency accepts in electronic form. This docket will identify specifically what types of documents or parts of documents are acceptable for submission in electronic form without paper records and the agency receiving unit(s) (e.g., specific center, office, division, branch) to which such submissions may be made. Documents to agency receiving unit(s) not specified in the public docket will not be considered as official if they are submitted in electronic form; paper forms of such documents will be considered as official and must accompany any electronic records. Persons are expected to consult with the intended agency receiving unit for details on how (e.g., method of transmission, media, file formats, and technical protocols) and whether to proceed with the electronic submission.

§11.3 Definitions.

(a) The definitions and interpretations of terms contained in section 201 of the act apply to those terms when used in this part.

(b) The following definitions of terms also apply to this part:

(1) *Act* means the Federal Food, Drug, and Cosmetic Act (§201-903 (21 U.S.C. 321-393)).

(2) *Agency* means the Food and Drug Administration.

(3) *Biometrics* means a method of verifying an individual's identity based on measurement of the individual's physical feature(s) or repeatable action(s) where those features and/or actions are both unique to that individual and measurable.

(4) *Closed system* means an environment in which system access is controlled by persons who are responsible for the content of electronic records that are on the system.

(5) *Digital signature* means an electronic signature based upon cryptographic methods of originator authentication, computed by using a set of rules and a set of parameters such that the identity of the signer and the integrity of the data can be verified.

(6) *Electronic record* means any combination of text, graphics, data, audio, pictorial, or other information representation in digital form that is created, modified, maintained, archived, retrieved, or distributed by a computer system.

(7) *Electronic signature* means a computer data compilation of any symbol or series of symbols executed, adopted, or authorized by an individual to be the legally binding equivalent of the individual's handwritten signature.

(8) *Handwritten signature* means the scripted name or legal mark of an individual handwritten by that individual and executed or adopted with the present intention to authenticate a writing in a permanent form. The act of signing with a writing or marking instrument such as a pen or stylus is preserved. The scripted name or legal mark,

while conventionally applied to paper, may also be applied to other devices that capture the name or mark.

(9) *Open system* means an environment in which system access is not controlled by persons who are responsible for the content of electronic records that are on the system.

Subpart B--Electronic Records

§11.10 Controls for closed systems.

Persons who use closed systems to create, modify, maintain, or transmit electronic records shall employ procedures and controls designed to ensure the authenticity, integrity, and, when appropriate, the confidentiality of electronic records, and to ensure that the signer cannot readily repudiate the signed record as not genuine. Such procedures and controls shall include the following:

(a) Validation of systems to ensure accuracy, reliability, consistent intended performance, and the ability to discern invalid or altered records.

(b) The ability to generate accurate and complete copies of records in both human readable and electronic form suitable for inspection, review, and copying by the agency. Persons should contact the agency if there are any questions regarding the ability of the agency to perform such review and copying of the electronic records.

(c) Protection of records to enable their accurate and ready retrieval throughout the records retention period.

(d) Limiting system access to authorized individuals.

(e) Use of secure, computer-generated, time-stamped audit trails to independently record the date and time of operator entries and actions that create, modify, or delete electronic records. Record changes shall not obscure previously recorded information. Such audit trail documentation shall be retained for a period at least as long as that required for the subject electronic records and shall be available for agency review and copying.

(f) Use of operational system checks to enforce permitted sequencing of steps and events, as appropriate.

(g) Use of authority checks to ensure that only authorized individuals can use the system, electronically sign a record, access the operation or computer system input or output device, alter a record, or perform the operation at hand.

(h) Use of device (e.g., terminal) checks to determine, as appropriate, the validity of the source of data input or operational instruction.

(i) Determination that persons who develop, maintain, or use electronic record/electronic signature systems have the education, training, and experience to perform their assigned tasks.

(j) The establishment of, and adherence to, written policies that hold individuals accountable and responsible for actions initiated under their electronic signatures, in order to deter record and signature falsification.

(k) Use of appropriate controls over systems documentation including:

(1) Adequate controls over the distribution of, access to, and use of documentation for system operation and maintenance.

(2) Revision and change control procedures to maintain an audit trail that documents time-sequenced development and modification of systems documentation.

§11.30   Controls for open systems.

Persons who use open systems to create, modify, maintain, or transmit electronic records shall employ procedures and controls designed to ensure the authenticity, integrity, and, as appropriate, the confidentiality of electronic records from the point of their creation to the point of their receipt. Such procedures and controls shall include those identified in §11.10, as appropriate, and additional measures such as document encryption and use of appropriate digital signature standards to ensure, as necessary under the circumstances, record authenticity, integrity, and confidentiality.

§11.50 Signature manifestations.

(a) Signed electronic records shall contain information associated with the signing that clearly indicates all of the following:

(1) The printed name of the signer;

(2) The date and time when the signature was executed; and

(3) The meaning (such as review, approval, responsibility, or authorship) associated with the signature.

(b) The items identified in paragraphs (a)(1), (a)(2), and (a)(3) of this section shall be subject to the same controls as for electronic records and shall be included as part of any human readable form of the electronic record (such as electronic display or printout).

§11.70 Signature/record linking.

Electronic signatures and handwritten signatures executed to electronic records shall be linked to their respective electronic records to ensure that the signatures cannot be excised, copied, or otherwise transferred to falsify an electronic record by ordinary means.

Subpart C--Electronic Signatures

§11.100 General requirements.

(a) Each electronic signature shall be unique to one individual and shall not be reused by, or reassigned to, anyone else.

(b) Before an organization establishes, assigns, certifies, or otherwise sanctions an individual's electronic signature, or any element of such electronic signature, the organization shall verify the identity of the individual.

(c) Persons using electronic signatures shall, prior to or at the time of such use, certify to the agency that the electronic signatures in their system, used on or after August 20, 1997, are intended to be the legally binding equivalent of traditional handwritten signatures.

(1) The certification shall be submitted in paper form and

signed with a traditional handwritten signature, to the Office of Regional Operations (HFC-100), 5600 Fishers Lane, Rockville, MD 20857.

(2) Persons using electronic signatures shall, upon agency request, provide additional certification or testimony that a specific electronic signature is the legally binding equivalent of the signer's handwritten signature.

§11.200 Electronic signature components and controls.

(a) Electronic signatures that are not based upon biometrics shall:

(1) Employ at least two distinct identification components such as an identification code and password.

(i) When an individual executes a series of signings during a single, continuous period of controlled system access, the first signing shall be executed using all electronic signature components; subsequent signings shall be executed using at least one electronic signature component that is only executable by, and designed to be used only by, the individual.

(ii) When an individual executes one or more signings not performed during a single, continuous period of controlled system access, each signing shall be executed using all of the electronic signature components.

(2) Be used only by their genuine owners; and

(3) Be administered and executed to ensure that attempted use of an individual's electronic signature by anyone other than its genuine owner requires collaboration of two or more individuals.

(b) Electronic signatures based upon biometrics shall be designed to ensure that they cannot be used by anyone other than their genuine owners.

§11.300 Controls for identification codes/passwords.

Persons who use electronic signatures based upon use of identification codes in combination with passwords shall employ controls to ensure their security and integrity. Such controls shall include:

(a) Maintaining the uniqueness of each combined identification code and password, such that no two individuals have the same combination of identification code and password.

(b) Ensuring that identification code and password issuances are periodically checked, recalled, or revised (e.g., to cover such events as password aging).

(c) Following loss management procedures to electronically deauthorize lost, stolen, missing, or otherwise potentially compromised tokens, cards, and other devices that bear or generate identification code or password information, and to issue temporary or permanent replacements using suitable, rigorous controls.

(d) Use of transaction safeguards to prevent unauthorized use of passwords and/or identification codes, and to detect and report in an immediate and urgent manner any attempts at their unauthorized use to the system security unit, and, as appropriate, to organizational management.

(e) Initial and periodic testing of devices, such as tokens or cards, that bear or generate identification code or password information to ensure that they function properly and have not been altered in an unauthorized manner.

Notes

Guidance for Industry
Part 11, Electronic Records; Electronic Signatures — Scope and Application

Office of Training and Communications
Division of Drug Information
Center for Drug Evaluation and Research (CDER)
WO51, Room 2201
10903 New Hampshire Ave
Silver Spring, MD 20993
Phone: 301-796-3400 Fax: 301-847-8714
E-mail: druginfo@fda.hhs.gov
http://www.fda.gov/Drugs/GuidanceComplianceRegulatoryInformation/Guidances/default.htm

or

Office of Communication, Training and
Manufacturers Assistance, HFM-40
Center for Biologics Evaluation and Research (CBER)
Phone: the Voice Information System at
800-835-4709 or 301-827-1800
http://www.fda.gov/BiologicsBloodVaccines/GuidanceComplianceRegulatoryInformation/Guidances/default.htm

or

Communications Staff (HFV-12),
Center for Veterinary Medicine (CVM)
(Tel) 240-276-9300
http://www.fda.gov/AnimalVeterinary/GuidanceComplianceEnforcement/GuidanceforIndustry/default.htm

or

Division of Small Manufacturers, International, and
Consumer Assistance (HFZ-220)
http://www.fda.gov/cdrh/ggpmain.html
Manufacturers Assistance Phone Number: 800-638-2041
or 301-796-7100

or

Center for Food Safety and Applied Nutrition (CFSAN)
http://www.fda.gov/Food/GuidanceRegulation/GuidanceDocumentsRegulatoryInformation/default.htm

U.S. Department of Health and Human Services
Food and Drug Administration
Center for Drug Evaluation and Research (CDER)
Center for Biologics Evaluation and Research (CBER)
Center for Devices and Radiological Health (CDRH)
Center for Food Safety and Applied Nutrition (CFSAN)
Center for Veterinary Medicine (CVM)
Office of Regulatory Affairs (ORA)

August 2003
Pharmaceutical CGMPs

TABLE OF CONTENTS

I. INTRODUCTION
II. BACKGROUND
III. DISCUSSION

A. Overall Approach to Part 11 Requirements

B. Details of Approach – Scope of Part 11
1. Narrow Interpretation of Scope
2. Definition of Part 11 Records

C. Approach to Specific Part 11 Requirements
1. Validation
2. Audit Trail
3. Legacy Systems
4. Copies of Records
5. Record Retention

IV. REFERENCES

Guidance for Industry[1]
Part 11, Electronic Records; Electronic Signatures Scope and Application
Contains Nonbinding RecommendationsM

This guidance represents the Food and Drug Administration's (FDA's) current thinking on this topic. It does not create or confer any rights for or on any person and does not operate to bind FDA or the public. You can use an alternative approach if the approach satisfies the requirements of the applicable statutes and regulations. If you want to discuss an alternative approach, contact the FDA staff responsible for implementing this guidance. If you cannot identify the appropriate FDA staff, call the appropriate number listed on the title page of this guidance.

I. INTRODUCTION

This guidance is intended to describe the Food and Drug Administration's (FDA's) current thinking regarding the scope and application of part 11 of Title 21 of the Code of Federal Regulations; Electronic Records; Electronic Signatures (21 CFR Part 11).[2]

This document provides guidance to persons who, in fulfillment of a requirement in a statute or another part of FDA's regulations to maintain records or submit information to FDA[3], have chosen to maintain the records or submit designated information electronically and, as a result, have become subject to part 11. Part 11 applies to records in electronic form that are created, modified, maintained, archived, retrieved, or transmitted under any records requirements set forth in Agency regulations. Part 11 also applies to electronic records submitted to the Agency under the Federal Food, Drug, and Cosmetic Act (the Act) and the Public Health Service Act (the PHS Act), even if such records are not specifically identified in Agency regulations (§ 11.1). The underlying requirements set forth in the Act, PHS Act, and FDA regulations (other than part 11) are referred to in this guidance document as *predicate rules*.

As an outgrowth of its current good manufacturing practice (CGMP) initiative for human and animal drugs and biologics,[4] FDA is re-examining part 11 as it applies to all FDA regulated products. We anticipate initiating rulemaking to change part 11 as a result of that re-examination. This guidance explains that we will narrowly interpret the scope of part 11. While the re-examination of part 11 is under way, we intend to exercise enforcement discretion with respect to certain part 11 requirements. That is, we do not intend to take enforcement action to enforce compliance with the validation, audit trail, record retention, and record copying requirements of part 11 as explained in this guidance. However, records must still be maintained or submitted in accordance with the underlying predicate rules, and the Agency can take regulatory action for noncompliance with such predicate rules.

In addition, we intend to exercise enforcement discretion and do not intend to take (or recommend) action to enforce any part 11 requirements with regard to systems that were operational before August 20, 1997, the effective date of part 11 (commonly known as legacy systems) under the circumstances described in section III.C.3 of this guidance.

Note that part 11 remains in effect and that this exercise of enforcement discretion applies only as identified in this guidance.

FDA's guidance documents, including this guidance, do not establish legally enforceable responsibilities. Instead, guidances describe the Agency's current thinking on a topic and should be viewed only as recommendations, unless specific regulatory or statutory requirements are cited. The use of the word should in Agency guidances means that something is suggested or recommended, but not required.

II. BACKGROUND

In March of 1997, FDA issued final part 11 regulations that provide criteria for acceptance by FDA, under certain circumstances, of electronic records, electronic signatures, and handwritten signatures executed to electronic records as equivalent to paper records and handwritten signatures executed on paper. These regulations, which apply to all FDA program areas, were intended to permit the widest possible use of electronic technology, compatible with FDA's responsibility to protect the public health.

After part 11 became effective in August 1997, significant discussions ensued among industry, contractors, and the Agency concerning the interpretation and implementation of the regulations. FDA has (1) spoken about part 11 at many conferences and met numerous times with an industry coalition and other interested parties in an effort to hear more about potential part 11 issues; (2) published a compliance policy guide, CPG 7153.17: Enforcement Policy: 21 CFR Part 11; Electronic Records; Electronic Signatures; and (3) published numerous draft guidance documents including the following:

• *21 CFR Part 11; Electronic Records; Electronic Signatures, Validation*

• *21 CFR Part 11; Electronic Records; Electronic Signatures, Glossary of Terms*

• *21 CFR Part 11; Electronic Records; Electronic Signatures, Time Stamps*

• *21 CFR Part 11; Electronic Records; Electronic Signatures, Maintenance of Electronic Records*

• *21 CFR Part 11; Electronic Records; Electronic Signatures, Electronic Copies of Electronic Records*

Throughout all of these communications, concerns have been raised that some interpretations of the part 11 requirements would (1) unnecessarily restrict the use of electronic technology in a manner that is inconsistent with FDA's stated intent in issuing the rule, (2) significantly increase the costs of compliance to an extent that was not contemplated at the time the rule was drafted, and (3) discourage innovation and technological advances without providing a significant public health benefit. These concerns have been raised particularly in the areas of part 11 requirements for validation, audit trails, record retention, record copying, and legacy systems.

As a result of these concerns, we decided to review the part 11 documents and related issues, particularly in light of the Agency's CGMP initiative. In the *Federal Register* of February 4, 2003 (68 FR 5645), we announced the withdrawal of the draft guidance for industry, *21 CFR Part 11; Electronic Records; Electronic Signatures, Electronic Copies of Electronic Records*. We had decided we wanted to minimize industry time spent reviewing and commenting on the draft guidance when that draft guidance may no longer represent our approach under the CGMP initiative. Then, in the *Federal Register* of February 25, 2003 (68 FR 8775), we announced the withdrawal of the part 11 draft guidance documents on validation, glossary of terms, time stamps,[5] maintenance of electronic records, and CPG 7153.17. We received valuable public comments on these draft guidances, and we plan to use that information to help with future decision-making with respect to part 11. We do not intend to re-issue these draft guidance documents or the CPG.

We are now re-examining part 11, and we anticipate initiating rulemaking to revise provisions of that regulation. To avoid unnecessary resource expenditures to comply with part 11 requirements, we are issuing this guidance to describe how we intend to exercise enforcement discretion with regard to certain part 11 requirements during the re-examination of part 11. As mentioned previously, part 11 remains in effect during this re-examination period.

III. DISCUSSION

A. Overall Approach to Part 11 Requirements

As described in more detail below, the approach outlined in this guidance is based on three main elements:

- Part 11 will be interpreted narrowly; we are now clarifying that fewer records will be considered subject to part 11.

- For those records that remain subject to part 11, we intend to exercise enforcement discretion with regard to part 11 requirements for validation, audit trails, record retention, and record copying in the manner described in this guidance and with regard to all part 11 requirements for systems that were operational before the effective date of part 11 (also known as legacy systems).

- We will enforce all predicate rule requirements, including predicate rule record and recordkeeping requirements.

It is important to note that FDA's exercise of enforcement discretion as described in this guidance is limited to specified part 11 requirements (setting aside legacy systems, as to which the extent of enforcement discretion, under certain circumstances, will be more broad). We intend to enforce all other provisions of part 11 including, but not limited to, certain controls for closed systems in §11.10. For example, we intend to enforce provisions related to the following controls and requirements:

- limiting system access to authorized individuals
- use of operational system checks
- use of authority checks
- use of device checks

- determination that persons who develop, maintain, or use electronic systems have the education, training, and experience to perform their assigned tasks

- establishment of and adherence to written policies that hold individuals accountable for actions initiated under their electronic signatures

- appropriate controls over systems documentation

- controls for open systems corresponding to controls for closed systems bulleted above (§ 11.30)

- requirements related to electronic signatures (e.g., §§11.50, 11.70, 11.100, 11.200, and 11.300)

We expect continued compliance with these provisions, and we will continue to enforce them. Furthermore, persons must comply with applicable predicate rules, and records that are required to be maintained or submitted must remain secure and reliable in accordance with the predicate rules.

B. Details of Approach – Scope of Part 11

1. Narrow Interpretation of Scope

We understand that there is some confusion about the scope of part 11. Some have understood the scope of part 11 to be very broad. We believe that some of those broad interpretations could lead to unnecessary controls and costs and could discourage innovation and technological advances without providing added benefit to the public health. As a result, we want to clarify that the Agency intends to interpret the scope of part 11 narrowly.

Under the narrow interpretation of the scope of part 11, with respect to records required to be maintained under predicate rules or submitted to FDA, when persons choose to use records in electronic format in place of paper format, part 11 would apply. On the other hand, when persons use computers to generate paper printouts of electronic records, and those paper records meet all the requirements of the applicable predicate rules and persons rely on the paper records to perform their regulated activities, FDA would generally not consider persons to be "using electronic records in lieu of paper records" under §§11.2(a) and 11.2(b). In these instances, the use of computer systems in the generation of paper records would not trigger part 11.

2. Definition of Part 11 Records

Under this narrow interpretation, FDA considers part 11 to be applicable to the following records or signatures in electronic format (part 11 records or signatures):

- Records that are required to be maintained under predicate rule requirements and that are maintained in electronic format *in place of paper format.* On the other hand, records (and any associated signatures) that are not required to be retained under predicate rules, but that are nonetheless maintained in electronic format, are not part 11 records.

We recommend that you determine, based on the predicate rules, whether specific records are part 11 records. We recommend that you document such decisions.

- Records that are required to be maintained under predicate rules, that are maintained in electronic format *in addition to paper format,* and that *are relied on to perform regulated activities.*

In some cases, actual business practices may dictate whether you are *using* electronic records instead of paper records under §11.2(a). For example, if a record is required to be maintained under a predicate rule and you use a computer to generate a paper printout of the electronic records, but you nonetheless rely on the electronic record to perform regulated activities, the Agency may consider you to be using the electronic record instead of the paper record. That is, the Agency may take your business practices into account in determining whether part 11 applies.

Accordingly, we recommend that, for each record required to be maintained under predicate rules, you determine in advance whether you plan to rely on the electronic record or paper record to perform regulated activities. We recommend that you document this decision (e.g., in a Standard Operating Procedure (SOP), or specification document).

- Records submitted to FDA, under predicate rules (even if such records are not specifically identified in Agency regulations) in electronic format (assuming the records have been identified in docket number 92S-0251 as the types of submissions the Agency accepts in electronic format). However, a record that is not itself submitted, but is used in generating a submission, is not a part 11 record unless it is otherwise required to be maintained under a predicate rule and it is maintained in electronic format.

• Electronic signatures that are intended to be the equivalent of handwritten signatures, initials, and other general signings required by predicate rules. Part 11 signatures include electronic signatures that are used, for example, to document the fact that certain events or actions occurred in accordance with the predicate rule (e.g. *approved, reviewed,* and *verified).*

C. Approach to Specific Part 11 Requirements

1. Validation

The Agency intends to exercise enforcement discretion regarding specific part 11 requirements for validation of computerized systems (§11.10(a) and corresponding requirements in §11.30). Although persons must still comply with all applicable predicate rule requirements for validation (e.g., 21 CFR 820.70(i)), this guidance should not be read to impose any additional requirements for validation.

We suggest that your decision to validate computerized systems, and the extent of the validation, take into account the impact the systems have on your ability to meet predicate rule requirements. You should also consider the impact those systems might have on the accuracy, reliability, integrity, availability, and authenticity of required records and signatures. Even if there is no predicate rule requirement to validate a system, in some instances it may still be important to validate the system.

We recommend that you base your approach on a justified and documented risk assessment and a determination of the potential of the system to affect product quality and safety, and record integrity. For instance, validation would not be important for a word processor used only to generate SOPs.

For further guidance on validation of computerized systems, see FDA's guidance for industry and FDA staff *General Principles of Software Validation* and also industry guidance such as the *GAMP 4 Guide* (See References).

2. Audit Trail

The Agency intends to exercise enforcement discretion regarding specific part 11 requirements related to computer-generated, time-stamped audit trails (§11.10 (e), (k)(2) and any corresponding requirement in §11.30). Persons must still comply with all applicable predicate rule requirements related to documentation of, for example, date (e.g., § 58.130(e)), time, or sequencing of events, as well as any requirements for ensuring that changes to records do not obscure previous entries.

Even if there are no predicate rule requirements to document, for example, date, time, or sequence of events in a particular instance, it may nonetheless be important to have audit trails or other physical, logical, or procedural security measures in place to ensure the trustworthiness and reliability of the records. [6]We recommend that you base your decision on whether to apply audit trails, or other appropriate measures, on the need to comply with predicate rule requirements, a justified and documented risk assessment, and a determination of the potential effect on product quality and safety and record integrity. We suggest that you apply appropriate controls based on such an assessment. Audit trails can be particularly appropriate when users are expected to create, modify, or delete regulated records during normal operation.

3. Legacy Systems[7]

The Agency intends to exercise enforcement discretion with respect to all part 11 requirements for systems that otherwise were operational prior to August 20, 1997, the effective date of part 11, under the circumstances specified below.

This means that the Agency does not intend to take enforcement action to enforce compliance with any part 11 requirements if all the following criteria are met for a specific system:

• The system was operational before the effective date.

• The system met all applicable predicate rule requirments before the effective date.

• The system currently meets all applicable predicate rule requirements.

• You have documented evidence and justification that the system is fit for its intended use (including having an acceptable level of record security and integrity, if applicable).

If a system has been changed since August 20, 1997, and if the changes would prevent the system from meeting predicate rule requirements, Part 11 controls should be applied to Part 11 records and signatures pursuant to the enforcement policy expressed in this guidance.

4. Copies of Records

The Agency intends to exercise enforcement discretion with regard to specific part 11 requirements for generating copies of records (§11.10 (b) and any corresponding requirement in §11.30). You should provide an investigator with reasonable and useful access to records during an inspection. All records held by you are subject to inspection in accordance with predicate rules (e.g.,§§ 211.180(c), (d), and 108.35(c)(3)(ii)).

We recommend that you supply copies of electronic records by:

• Producing copies of records held in common portable formats when records are maintained in these formats

• Using established automated conversion or export methods, where available, to make copies in a more common format (examples of such formats include, but are not limited to, PDF, XML, or SGML)

In each case, we recommend that the copying process used produces copies that preserve the content and meaning of the record. If you have the ability to search, sort, or trend part 11 records, copies given to the Agency should provide the same capability if it is reasonable and technically feasible. You should allow inspection, review, and copying of records in a human readable form at your site using your hardware and following your established procedures and techniques for accessing records.

5. Record Retention

The Agency intends to exercise enforcement discretion with regard to the part 11 requirements for the protection of records to enable their accurate and ready retrieval throughout the records retention period (§11.10 (c) and any corresponding requirement in §11.30). Persons must still comply with all applicable predicate rule requirements for record retention and availability (e.g., §§ 211.180(c),(d), 108.25(g), and 108.35(h)).

We suggest that your decision on how to maintain records be based on predicate rule requirements and that you base your decision on a justified and documented risk assessment and a determination of the value of the records over time.

FDA does not intend to object if you decide to archive required records in electronic format to nonelectronic media such as microfilm, microfiche, and paper, or to a standard electronic file format (examples of such formats include, but are not limited to, PDF, XML, or SGML). Persons must still comply with all predicate rule requirements, and the records themselves and any copies of the required records should preserve their content and meaning. As long as predicate rule requirements are fully satisfied and the content and meaning of the records are preserved and archived, you can delete the electronic version of the records. In addition, paper and electronic record and signature components can co-exist (i.e., a hybrid[8] situation) as long as predicate rule requirements are met and the content and meaning of those records are preserved.

IV. REFERENCES

Food and Drug Administration References

1. *Glossary of Computerized System and Software Development Terminology* (Division of Field Investigations, Office of Regional Operations, Office of Regulatory Affairs, FDA 1995) (http://www.fda.gov/ora/inspect_ref/igs/gloss.html)

2. *General Principles of Software Validation*; Final Guidance for Industry and FDA Staff (FDA, Center for Devices and Radiological Health, Center for Biologics Evaluation and Research, 2002) (http://www.fda.gov/cdrh/comp/guidance/938.html)

3. *Guidance for Industry, FDA Reviewers, and Compliance on Off-The-Shelf Software Use in Medical Devices* (FDA, Center for Devices and Radiological Health, 1999) (http://www.fda.gov/cdrh/ode/guidance/585.html)

4. *Pharmaceutical CGMPs for the 21st Century: A Risk-Based Approach*; A Science and Risk-Based Approach to Product Quality Regulation Incorporating an Integrated Quality Systems Approach (FDA 2002) (http://www.fda.gov/oc/guidance/gmp.html)

Industry References

1. *The Good Automated Manufacturing Practice (GAMP) Guide for Validation of Automated Systems, GAMP 4* (ISPE/GAMP Forum, 2001) (http://www.ispe.org/gamp/)

2. ISO/IEC 17799:2000 (BS 7799:2000) Information technology - Code of practice for information security management (ISO/IEC, 2000)

3. ISO 14971:2002 Medical Devices- Application of risk management to medical devices (ISO, 2001)

[1] This guidance has been prepared by the Office of Compliance in the Center for Drug Evaluation and Research (CDER) in consultation with the other Agency centers and the Office of Regulatory Affairs at the Food and Drug Administration.

[2] 62 FR 13430

[3] These requirements include, for example, certain provisions of the Current Good Manufacturing Practice regulations (21 CFR Part 211), the Quality System regulation (21 CFR Part 820), and the Good Laboratory Practice for Nonclinical Laboratory Studies regulations (21 CFR Part 58).

[4] See Pharmaceutical CGMPs for the 21st Century: A Risk-Based Approach; A Science and Risk-Based Approach to Product Quality Regulation Incorporating an Integrated Quality Systems Approach at www.fda.gov/oc/guidance/gmp.html.

[5] Although we withdrew the draft guidance on time stamps, our current thinking has not changed in that when using time stamps for systems that span different time zones, we do not expect you to record the signer's local time. When using time stamps, they should be implemented with a clear understanding of the time zone reference used. In such instances, system documentation should explain time zone references as well as zone acronyms or other naming conventions.

[6] Various guidance documents on information security are available (see References).

[7] In this guidance document, we use the term legacy system to describe systems already in operation before the effective date of part 11.

[8] Examples of hybrid situations include combinations of paper records (or other nonelectronic media) and electronic records, paper records and electronic signatures, or handwritten signatures executed to electronic records.

Notes

Parts 210 & 211

The Code of Federal Regulations
Title 21 – Food and Drugs

Parts 210 & 211
cGMP in Manufacturing, Processing, Packing, or Holding of Drugs and Finished Pharmaceuticals

---

Printed by GMP Publications, Inc.
Tel: 866-544-9007 or 856-810-7331
Fax: 866-544-9002
http://www.gmppublications.com
sales@gmppublications.com

PART 210--CURRENT GOOD MANUFACTURING PRACTICE IN MANUFACTURING, PROCESSING, PACKING, OR HOLDING OF DRUGS; GENERAL

§210.1 Status of current good manufacturing practice regulations.
§210.2 Applicability of current good manufacturing practice regulations.
§210.3 Definitions.

Authority: 21 U.S.C. 321, 351, 352, 355, 360b, 371, 374; 42 U.S.C. 216, 262, 263a, 264.

Source: 43 FR 45076, Sept, 29, 1978, unless otherwise noted.

§210.1 Status of current good manufacturing practice regulations.

(a) The regulations set forth in this part and in parts 211, 225, and 226 of this chapter contain the minimum current good manufacturing practice for methods to be used in, and the facilities or controls to be used for, the manufacture, processing, packing, or holding of a drug to assure that such drug meets the requirements of the act as to safety, and has the identity and strength and meets the quality and purity characteristics that it purports or is represented to possess.

(b) The failure to comply with any regulation set forth in this part and in parts 211, 225, and 226 of this chapter in the manufacture, processing, packing, or holding of a drug shall render such drug to be adulterated under section 501(a)(2)(B) of the act and such drug, as well as the person who is responsible for the failure to comply, shall be subject to regulatory action.

(c) Owners and operators of establishments engaged in the recovery, donor screening, testing (including donor testing), processing, storage, labeling, packaging, or distribution of human cells, tissues, and cellular and tissue-based products (HCT/Ps), as defined in §1271.3(d) of this chapter, that are drugs (subject to review under an application submitted under section 505 of the act or under a biological product license application under section 351 of the Public Health Service Act), are subject to the donor-eligibility and applicable current good tissue practice procedures set forth in part 1271 subparts C and D of this chapter, in addition to the regulations in this part and in parts 211, 225, and 226 of this chapter. Failure to comply with any applicable regulation set forth in this part, in parts 211, 225, and 226 of this chapter, in part 1271 subpart C of this chapter, or in part 1271 subpart D of this chapter with respect to the manufacture, processing, packing or holding of a drug, renders an HCT/P adulterated under section 501(a)(2)(B) of the act. Such HCT/P, as well as the person who is responsible for the failure to comply, is subject to regulatory action.

[43 FR 45076, Sept. 29, 1978, as amended at 69 FR 29828, May 25, 2004; 74 FR 65431, Dec. 10, 2009]

§210.2 Applicability of current good manufacturing practice regulations.

(a) The regulations in this part and in parts 211, 225, and 226 of this chapter as they may pertain to a drug; in parts 600 through 680 of this chapter as they may pertain to a biological product for human use; and in part 1271 of this chapter as they are applicable to a human cell, tissue, or cellular or tissue-based product (HCT/P) that is a drug (subject to review under an application submitted under section 505 of the act or under a biological product license application under section 351 of the Public Health Service Act); shall be considered to supplement, not supersede, each other, unless the regulations explicitly provide otherwise. In the event of a conflict between applicable regulations in this part and in other parts of this chapter, the regulation specifically applicable to the drug product in question shall supersede the more general.

(b) If a person engages in only some operations subject to the regulations in this part, in parts 211, 225, and 226 of this chapter, in parts 600 through 680 of this chapter, and in part 1271 of this chapter, and not in others, that person need only comply with those regulations applicable to the operations in which he or she is engaged.

(c) An investigational drug for use in a phase 1 study, as described in §312.21(a) of this chapter, is subject to the statutory requirements set forth in 21 U.S.C. 351(a)(2)(B). The production of such drug is exempt from compliance with the regulations in part 211 of this chapter. However, this exemption does not apply to an investigational drug for use in a phase 1 study once the investigational drug has been made available for use by or for the sponsor in a phase 2 or phase 3 study, as described in §312.21(b) and (c) of this chapter, or the drug has been lawfully marketed. If the investigational drug has been made available in a phase 2 or phase 3 study or the drug has been lawfully marketed, the drug for use in the phase 1 study must comply with part 211.

[69 FR 29828, May 25, 2004, as amended at 73 FR 40462, July 15, 2008; 74 FR 65431, Dec. 10, 2009]

§210.3　　Definitions.

(a) The definitions and interpretations contained in section 201 of the act shall be applicable to such terms when used in this part and in parts 211, 225, and 226 of this chapter.

(b) The following definitions of terms apply to this part and to parts 211 through 226 of this chapter.

(1) *Act* means the Federal Food, Drug, and Cosmetic Act, as amended (21 U.S.C. 301 *et seq.*).

(2) *Batch* means a specific quantity of a drug or other material that is intended to have uniform character and quality, within specified limits, and is produced according to a single manufacturing order during the same cycle of manufacture.

(3) *Component* means any ingredient intended for use in the manufacture of a drug product, including those that may not appear in such drug product.

(4) *Drug product* means a finished dosage form, for example, tablet, capsule, solution, etc., that contains an active drug ingredient generally, but not necessarily, in association with inactive ingredients. The term also includes a finished dosage form that does not contain an active ingredient but is intended to be used as a placebo.

(5) *Fiber* means any particulate contaminant with a length at least three times greater than its width.

(6) *Nonfiber releasing filter* means any filter, which after appropriate pretreatment such as washing or flushing,

will not release fibers into the component or drug product that is being filtered.

(7) *Active ingredient* means any component that is intended to furnish pharmacological activity or other direct effect in the diagnosis, cure, mitigation, treatment, or prevention of disease, or to affect the structure or any function of the body of man or other animals. The term includes those components that may undergo chemical change in the manufacture of the drug product and be present in the drug product in a modified form intended to furnish the specified activity or effect.

(8) *Inactive ingredient* means any component other than an active ingredient.

(9) *In-process material* means any material fabricated, compounded, blended, or derived by chemical reaction that is produced for, and used in, the preparation of the drug product.

(10) *Lot* means a batch, or a specific identified portion of a batch, having uniform character and quality within specified limits; or, in the case of a drug product produced by continuous process, it is a specific identified amount produced in a unit of time or quantity in a manner that assures its having uniform character and quality within specified limits.

(11) *Lot number, control number, or batch number* means any distinctive combination of letters, numbers, or symbols, or any combination of them, from which the complete history of the manufacture, processing, packing, holding, and distribution of a batch or lot of drug product or other material can be determined.

(12) *Manufacture, processing, packing, or holding of a drug product* includes packaging and labeling operations, testing, and quality control of drug products.

(13) The term *medicated feed* means any Type B or Type C medicated feed as defined in §558.3 of this chapter. The feed contains one or more drugs as defined in section 201(q) of the act. The manufacture of medicated feeds is subject to the requirements of part 225 of this chapter.

(14) The term *medicated premix* means a Type A medicated article as defined in §558.3 of this chapter. The article contains one or more drugs as defined in section

201(g) of the act. The manufacture of medicated premixes is subject to the requirements of part 226 of this chapter.

(15) *Quality control unit* means any person or organizational element designated by the firm to be responsible for the duties relating to quality control.

(16) *Strength* means:

(i) The concentration of the drug substance (for example, weight/weight, weight/volume, or unit dose/volume basis), and/or

(ii) The potency, that is, the therapeutic activity of the drug product as indicated by appropriate laboratory tests or by adequately developed and controlled clinical data (expressed, for example, in terms of units by reference to a standard).

(17) *Theoretical yield* means the quantity that would be produced at any appropriate phase of manufacture, processing, or packing of a particular drug product, based upon the quantity of components to be used, in the absence of any loss or error in actual production.

(18) *Actual yield* means the quantity that is actually produced at any appropriate phase of manufacture, processing, or packing of a particular drug product.

(19) *Percentage of theoretical yield* means the ratio of the actual yield (at any appropriate phase of manufacture, processing, or packing of a particular drug product) to the theoretical yield (at the same phase), stated as a percentage.

(20) *Acceptance criteria* means the product specifications and acceptance/rejection criteria, such as acceptable quality level and unacceptable quality level, with an associated sampling plan, that are necessary for making a decision to accept or reject a lot or batch (or any other convenient subgroups of manufactured units).

(21) *Representative sample* means a sample that consists of a number of units that are drawn based on rational criteria such as random sampling and intended to assure that the sample accurately portrays the material being sampled.

(22) *Gang-printed labeling* means labeling derived from a sheet of material on which more than one item of labeling is printed.

[43 FR 45076, Sept. 29, 1978, as amended at 51 FR 7389, Mar. 3, 1986; 58 FR 41353, Aug. 3, 1993; 73 FR 51931, Sept. 8, 2008; 74 FR 65431, Dec. 10, 2009]

PART 211--CURRENT GOOD MANUFACTURING PRACTICE FOR FINISHED PHARMACEUTICALS

Subpart A--General Provisions

§211.1 Scope.
§211.3 Definitions.

Subpart B--Organization and Personnel

§211.22 Responsibilities of quality control unit.
§211.25 Personnel qualifications.
§211.28 Personnel responsibilities.
§211.34 Consultants.

Subpart C--Buildings and Facilities

§211.42 Design and construction features.
§211.44 Lighting.
§211.46 Ventilation, air filtration, air heating and cooling.
§211.48 Plumbing.
§211.50 Sewage and refuse.
§211.52 Washing and toilet facilities.
§211.56 Sanitation.
§211.58 Maintenance.

Subpart D--Equipment

§211.63 Equipment design, size, and location.
§211.65 Equipment construction.
§211.67 Equipment cleaning and maintenance.
§211.68 Automatic, mechanical, and electronic equipment.
§211.72 Filters.

Subpart E--Control of Components and Drug Product Containers and Closures

§211.80 General requirements.
§211.82 Receipt and storage of untested components, drug product containers, and closures.

§211.84	Testing and approval or rejection of components, drug product containers, and closures.
§211.86	Use of approved components, drug product containers, and closures.
§211.87	Retesting of approved components, drug product containers, and closures.
§211.89	Rejected components, drug product containers, and closures.
§211.94	Drug product containers and closures.

Subpart F--Production and Process Controls

§211.100	Written procedures; deviations.
§211.101	Charge-in of components.
§211.103	Calculation of yield.
§211.105	Equipment identification.
§211.110	Sampling and testing of in-process materials and drug products.
§211.111	Time limitations on production.
§211.113	Control of microbiological contamination.
§211.115	Reprocessing.

Subpart G--Packaging and Labeling Control

§211.122	Materials examination and usage criteria.
§211.125	Labeling issuance.
§211.130	Packaging and labeling operations.
§211.132	Tamper-evident packaging requirements for over-the-counter (OTC) human drug products.
§211.134	Drug product inspection.
§211.137	Expiration dating.

Subpart H--Holding and Distribution

§211.142	Warehousing procedures.
§211.150	Distribution procedures.

Subpart I--Laboratory Controls

§211.160	General requirements.
§211.165	Testing and release for distribution.

§211.166　Stability testing.
§211.167　Special testing requirements.
§211.170　Reserve samples.
§211.173　Laboratory animals.
§211.176　Penicillin contamination.

Subpart J--Records and Reports

§211.180　General requirements.
§211.182　Equipment cleaning and use log.
§211.184　Component, drug product container, closure, and labeling records.
§211.186　Master production and control records.
§211.188　Batch production and control records.
§211.192　Production record review.
§211.194　Laboratory records.
§211.196　Distribution records.
§211.198　Complaint files.

Subpart K--Returned and Salvaged Drug Products

§211.204　Returned drug products.
§211.208　Drug product salvaging.

Authority: 21 U.S.C. 321, 351, 352, 355, 360b, 371, 374; 42 U.S.C. 216, 262, 263a, 264.

Source: 43 FR 45077, Sept. 29, 1978, unless otherwise noted.

Subpart A--General Provisions

§211.1   Scope.

(a) The regulations in this part contain the minimum current good manufacturing practice for preparation of drug products (excluding positron emission tomography drugs) for administration to humans or animals.

(b) The current good manufacturing practice regulations in this chapter as they pertain to drug products; in parts 600 through 680 of this chapter, as they pertain to drugs that are also biological products for human use; and in part 1271 of this chapter, as they are applicable to drugs that are also human cells, tissues, and cellular and tissue-based products (HCT/Ps) and that are drugs (subject to review under an application submitted under section 505 of the act or under a biological product license application under section 351 of the Public Health Service Act); supplement and do not supersede the regulations in this part unless the regulations explicitly provide otherwise. In the event of a conflict between applicable regulations in this part and in other parts of this chapter, or in parts 600 through 680 of this chapter, or in part 1271 of this chapter, the regulation specifically applicable to the drug product in question shall supersede the more general.

(c) Pending consideration of a proposed exemption, published in the FEDERAL REGISTER of September 29, 1978, the requirements in this part shall not be enforced for OTC drug products if the products and all their ingredients are ordinarily marketed and consumed as human foods, and which products may also fall within the legal definition of drugs by virtue of their intended use. Therefore, until further notice, regulations under parts 110 and 117 of this chapter, and where applicable, parts 113 through 129 of this chapter, shall be applied in determining whether these OTC drug products that are also foods are manufactured, processed, packed, or held under current good manufacturing practice.

[43 FR 45077, Sept. 29, 1978, as amended at 62 FR 66522, Dec. 19, 1997; 69 FR 29828, May 25, 2004; 74 FR 65431, Dec. 10, 2009; 80 FR 56168, Sept. 17, 2015]

§211.3 Definitions.

The definitions set forth in §210.3 of this chapter apply in this part.

Subpart B--Organization and Personnel

§211.22 Responsibilities of quality control unit.

(a) There shall be a quality control unit that shall have the responsibility and authority to approve or reject all components, drug product containers, closures, in-process materials, packaging material, labeling, and drug products, and the authority to review production records to assure that no errors have occurred or, if errors have occurred, that they have been fully investigated. The quality control unit shall be responsible for approving or rejecting drug products manufactured, processed, packed, or held under contract by another company.

(b) Adequate laboratory facilities for the testing and approval (or rejection) of components, drug product containers, closures, packaging materials, in-process materials, and drug products shall be available to the quality control unit.

(c) The quality control unit shall have the responsibility for approving or rejecting all procedures or specifications impacting on the identity, strength, quality, and purity of the drug product.

(d) The responsibilities and procedures applicable to the quality control unit shall be in writing; such written procedures shall be followed.

§211.25 Personnel qualifications.

(a) Each person engaged in the manufacture, processing, packing, or holding of a drug product shall have education, training, and experience, or any combination thereof, to enable that person to perform the assigned functions. Training shall be in the particular operations that the employee performs and in current good manufacturing practice (including the current good manufacturing practice regulations in this chapter and written procedures required by these regulations) as they relate to the employee's functions. Training in current good manufacturing practice shall be conducted by qualified individuals on a continuing basis and with sufficient frequency to assure that employees remain familiar with CGMP requirements applicable to them.

(b) Each person responsible for supervising the manufacture, processing, packing, or holding of a drug product shall have the education, training, and experience, or any combination thereof, to perform assigned functions in such a manner as to provide assurance that the drug product has the safety, identity, strength, quality, and purity that it purports or is represented to possess.

(c) There shall be an adequate number of qualified personnel to perform and supervise the manufacture, processing, packing, or holding of each drug product.

§211.28 Personnel responsibilities.

(a) Personnel engaged in the manufacture, processing, packing, or holding of a drug product shall wear clean clothing appropriate for the duties they perform. Protective apparel, such as head, face, hand, and arm coverings, shall be worn as necessary to protect drug products from contamination.

(b) Personnel shall practice good sanitation and health habits.

(c) Only personnel authorized by supervisory personnel shall enter those areas of the buildings and facilities designated as limited-access areas.

d) Any person shown at any time (either by medical examination or supervisory observation) to have an apparent illness or open lesions that may adversely affect the safety or quality of drug products shall be excluded from direct contact with components, drug product containers, closures, in-process materials, and drug products until the condition is corrected or determined by competent medical personnel not to jeopardize the safety or quality of drug products. All personnel shall be instructed to report to supervisory personnel any health conditions that may have an adverse effect on drug products.

§211.34 Consultants.

Consultants advising on the manufacture, processing, packing, or holding of drug products shall have sufficient education, training, and experience, or any combination thereof, to advise on the subject for which they are retained. Records shall be maintained stating the name, address, and qualifications of any consultants and the type of service they provide.

Subpart C--Buildings and Facilities

§211.42 Design and construction features.

(a) Any building or buildings used in the manufacture, processing, packing, or holding of a drug product shall be of suitable size, construction and location to facilitate cleaning, maintenance, and proper operations.

(b) Any such building shall have adequate space for the orderly placement of equipment and materials to prevent mixups between different components, drug product containers, closures, labeling, in-process materials, or drug products, and to prevent contamination. The flow of components, drug product containers, closures, labeling, in-process materials, and drug products through the building or buildings shall be designed to prevent contamination.

(c) Operations shall be performed within specifically defined areas of adequate size. There shall be separate or defined areas or such other control systems for the firm's operations as are necessary to prevent contamination or mixups during the course of the following procedures:

(1) Receipt, identification, storage, and withholding from use of components, drug product containers, closures, and labeling, pending the appropriate sampling, testing, or examination by the quality control unit before release for manufacturing or packaging;

(2) Holding rejected components, drug product containers, closures, and labeling before disposition;

(3) Storage of released components, drug product containers, closures, and labeling;

(4) Storage of in-process materials;

(5) Manufacturing and processing operations;

(6) Packaging and labeling operations;
(7) Quarantine storage before release of drug products;
(8) Storage of drug products after release;
(9) Control and laboratory operations;
(10) Aseptic processing, which includes as appropriate:
(i) Floors, walls, and ceilings of smooth, hard surfaces that are easily cleanable;
(ii) Temperature and humidity controls;
(iii) An air supply filtered through high-efficiency particulate air filters under positive pressure, regardless of whether flow is laminar or nonlaminar;
(iv) A system for monitoring environmental conditions;
(v) A system for cleaning and disinfecting the room and equipment to produce aseptic conditions;
(vi) A system for maintaining any equipment used to control the aseptic conditions.
(d) Operations relating to the manufacture, processing, and packing of penicillin shall be performed in facilities separate from those used for other drug products for human use.

[43 FR 45077, Sept. 29, 1978, as amended at 60 FR 4091, Jan. 20, 1995]

§211.44　　Lighting.

Adequate lighting shall be provided in all areas.

§211.46　　Ventilation, air filtration, air heating and cooling.

(a) Adequate ventilation shall be provided.
(b) Equipment for adequate control over air pressure, micro-organisms, dust, humidity, and temperature shall be provided when appropriate for the manufacture, processing, packing, or holding of a drug product.
(c) Air filtration systems, including prefilters and particulate matter air filters, shall be used when appropriate on air supplies to production areas. If air is recirculated to production areas, measures shall be taken to control recirculation of dust from production. In areas where air contamination occurs during production, there shall be adequate exhaust systems or other systems adequate to control contaminants.

(d) Air-handling systems for the manufacture, processing, and packing of penicillin shall be completely separate from those for other drug products for human use.

§211.48 Plumbing.

(a) Potable water shall be supplied under continuous positive pressure in a plumbing system free of defects that could contribute contamination to any drug product. Potable water shall meet the standards prescribed in the Environmental Protection Agency's Primary Drinking Water Regulations set forth in 40 CFR part 141. Water not meeting such standards shall not be permitted in the potable water system.

(b) Drains shall be of adequate size and, where connected directly to a sewer, shall be provided with an air break or other mechanical device to prevent back-siphonage.

[43 FR 45077, Sept. 29, 1978, as amended at 48 FR 11426, Mar. 18, 1983]

§211.50 Sewage and refuse.

Sewage, trash, and other refuse in and from the building and immediate premises shall be disposed of in a safe and sanitary manner.

§211.52 Washing and toilet facilities.

Adequate washing facilities shall be provided, including hot and cold water, soap or detergent, air driers or single-service towels, and clean toilet facilities easily accessible to working areas.

§211.56 Sanitation.

(a) Any building used in the manufacture, processing, packing, or holding of a drug product shall be maintained in a clean and sanitary condition, Any such building shall be free of infestation by rodents, birds, insects, and other vermin (other than laboratory animals). Trash and organic waste matter shall be held and disposed of in a timely and sanitary manner.

(b) There shall be written procedures assigning responsibility for sanitation and describing in sufficient detail the cleaning schedules, methods, equipment, and materials to be used in cleaning the buildings and facilities; such written procedures shall be followed.

(c) There shall be written procedures for use of suitable rodenticides, insecticides, fungicides, fumigating agents, and cleaning and sanitizing agents. Such written procedures shall be designed to prevent the contamination of equipment, components, drug product containers, closures, packaging, labeling materials, or drug products and shall be followed. Rodenticides, insecticides, and fungicides shall not be used unless registered and used in accordance with the Federal Insecticide, Fungicide, and Rodenticide Act (7 U.S.C. 135).

(d) Sanitation procedures shall apply to work performed by contractors or temporary employees as well as work performed by full-time employees during the ordinary course of operations.

§211.58 Maintenance.

Any building used in the manufacture, processing, packing, or holding of a drug product shall be maintained in a good state of repair.

Subpart D--Equipment

§211.63 Equipment design, size, and location.

Equipment used in the manufacture, processing, packing, or holding of a drug product shall be of appropriate design, adequate size, and suitably located to facilitate operations for its intended use and for its cleaning and maintenance.

§211.65 Equipment construction.

(a) Equipment shall be constructed so that surfaces that contact components, in-process materials, or drug products shall not be reactive, additive, or absorptive so as to alter the safety, identity, strength, quality, or purity of the drug product beyond the official or other established requirements.

(b) Any substances required for operation, such as lubricants or coolants, shall not come into contact with components, drug product containers, closures, in-process materials, or drug products so as to alter the safety, identity, strength, quality, or purity of the drug product beyond the official or other established requirements.

§211.67   Equipment cleaning and maintenance.

(a) Equipment and utensils shall be cleaned, maintained, and, as appropriate for the nature of the drug, sanitized and/or sterilized at appropriate intervals to prevent malfunctions or contamination that would alter the safety, identity, strength, quality, or purity of the drug product beyond the official or other established requirements.

(b) Written procedures shall be established and followed for cleaning and maintenance of equipment, including utensils, used in the manufacture, processing, packing, or holding of a drug product. These procedures shall include, but are not necessarily limited to, the following:

(1) Assignment of responsibility for cleaning and maintaining equipment;

(2) Maintenance and cleaning schedules, including, where appropriate, sanitizing schedules;

(3) A description in sufficient detail of the methods, equipment, and materials used in cleaning and maintenance operations, and the methods of disassembling and reassembling equipment as necessary to assure proper cleaning and maintenance;

(4) Removal or obliteration of previous batch identification;

(5) Protection of clean equipment from contamination prior to use;

(6) Inspection of equipment for cleanliness immediately before use.

(c) Records shall be kept of maintenance, cleaning, sanitizing, and inspection as specified in §§211.180 and 211.182.

[43 FR 45077, Sept. 29, 1978, as amended at 73 FR 51931, Sept. 8, 2008]

§211.68 Automatic, mechanical, and electronic equipment.

(a) Automatic, mechanical, or electronic equipment or other types of equipment, including computers, or related systems that will perform a function satisfactorily, may be used in the manufacture, processing, packing, and holding of a drug product. If such equipment is so used, it shall be routinely calibrated, inspected, or checked according to a written program designed to assure proper performance. Written records of those calibration checks and inspections shall be maintained.

(b) Appropriate controls shall be exercised over computer or related systems to assure that changes in master production and control records or other records are instituted only by authorized personnel. Input to and output from the computer or related system of formulas or other records or data shall be checked for accuracy. The degree and frequency of input/output verification shall be based on the complexity and reliability of the computer or related system. A backup file of data entered into the computer or related system shall be maintained except where certain data, such as calculations performed in connection with laboratory analysis, are eliminated by computerization or other automated processes. In such instances a written record of the program shall be maintained along with appropriate validation data. Hard copy or alternative systems, such as duplicates, tapes, or microfilm, designed to assure that backup data are exact and complete and that it is secure from alteration, inadvertent erasures, or loss shall be maintained.

(c) Such automated equipment used for performance of operations addressed by §§211.101(c) or (d), 211.103, 211.182, or 211.188(b)(11) can satisfy the requirements included in those sections relating to the performance of an operation by one person and checking by another person if such equipment is used in conformity with this section, and one person checks that the equipment properly performed the operation.

[43 FR 45077, Sept. 29, 1978, as amended at 60 FR 4091, Jan. 20, 1995; 73 FR 51932, Sept. 8, 2008]

§211.72 Filters.

Filters for liquid filtration used in the manufacture, processing, or packing of injectable drug products intended for human use shall not release fibers into such products. Fiber-releasing filters may be used when it is not possible to manufacture such products without the use of these filters. If use of a fiber-releasing filter is necessary, an additional nonfiber-releasing filter having a maximum nominal pore size rating of 0.2 micron (0.45 micron if the manufacturing conditions so dictate) shall subsequently be used to reduce the content of particles in the injectable drug product. The use of an asbestos-containing filter is prohibited.

[73 FR 51932, Sept. 8, 2008]

Subpart E--Control of Components and Drug Product Containers and Closures

§211.80 General requirements.

(a) There shall be written procedures describing in sufficient detail the receipt, identification, storage, handling, sampling, testing, and approval or rejection of components and drug product containers and closures; such written procedures shall be followed.

(b) Components and drug product containers and closures shall at all times be handled and stored in a manner to prevent contamination.

(c) Bagged or boxed components of drug product containers, or closures shall be stored off the floor and suitably spaced to permit cleaning and inspection.

(d) Each container or grouping of containers for components or drug product containers, or closures shall be identified with a distinctive code for each lot in each shipment received. This code shall be used in recording the disposition of each lot. Each lot shall be appropriately identified as to its status (i.e., quarantined, approved, or rejected).

§211.82 Receipt and storage of untested components, drug product containers, and closures.

(a) Upon receipt and before acceptance, each container or grouping of containers of components, drug product containers, and closures shall be examined visually for appropriate labeling as to contents, container damage or broken seals, and contamination.

(b) Components, drug product containers, and closures shall be stored under quarantine until they have been tested or examined, whichever is appropriate, and released. Storage within the area shall conform to the requirements of §211.80.

[43 FR 45077, Sept. 29, 1978, as amended at 73 FR 51932, Sept. 8, 2008]

§211.84 Testing and approval or rejection of components, drug product containers, and closures.

(a) Each lot of components, drug product containers, and closures shall be withheld from use until the lot has been sampled, tested, or examined, as appropriate, and released for use by the quality control unit.

(b) Representative samples of each shipment of each lot shall be collected for testing or examination. The number of containers to be sampled, and the amount of material to be taken from each container, shall be based upon appropriate criteria such as statistical criteria for component variability, confidence levels, and degree of precision desired, the past quality history of the supplier, and the quantity needed for analysis and reserve where required by §211.170.

(c) Samples shall be collected in accordance with the following procedures:

(1) The containers of components selected shall be cleaned when necessary in a manner to prevent introduction of contaminants into the component.

(2) The containers shall be opened, sampled, and resealed in a manner designed to prevent contamination of

their contents and contamination of other components, drug product containers, or closures.

(3) Sterile equipment and aseptic sampling techniques shall be used when necessary.

(4) If it is necessary to sample a component from the top, middle, and bottom of its container, such sample subdivisions shall not be composited for testing.

(5) Sample containers shall be identified so that the following information can be determined: name of the material sampled, the lot number, the container from which the sample was taken, the date on which the sample was taken, and the name of the person who collected the sample.

(6) Containers from which samples have been taken shall be marked to show that samples have been removed from them.

(d) Samples shall be examined and tested as follows:

(1) At least one test shall be conducted to verify the identity of each component of a drug product. Specific identity tests, if they exist, shall be used.

(2) Each component shall be tested for conformity with all appropriate written specifications for purity, strength, and quality. In lieu of such testing by the manufacturer, a report of analysis may be accepted from the supplier of a component, provided that at least one specific identity test is conducted on such component by the manufacturer, and provided that the manufacturer establishes the reliability of the supplier's analyses through appropriate validation of the supplier's test results at appropriate intervals.

(3) Containers and closures shall be tested for conformity with all appropriate written specifications. In lieu of such testing by the manufacturer, a certificate of testing may be accepted from the supplier, provided that at least a visual identification is conducted on such containers/closures by the manufacturer and provided that the manufacturer establishes the reliability of the supplier's test results through appropriate validation of the supplier's test results at appropriate intervals.

(4) When appropriate, components shall be microscopically examined.

(5) Each lot of a component, drug product container, or closure that is liable to contamination with filth, insect infestation, or other extraneous adulterant shall be examined against established specifications for such contamination.

(6) Each lot of a component, drug product container, or closure with potential for microbiological contamination that is objectionable in view of its intended use shall be subjected to microbiological tests before use.

(e) Any lot of components, drug product containers, or closures that meets the appropriate written specifications of identity, strength, quality, and purity and related tests under paragraph (d) of this section may be approved and released for use. Any lot of such material that does not meet such specifications shall be rejected.

[43 FR 45077, Sept. 29, 1978, as amended at 63 FR 14356, Mar. 25, 1998; 73 FR 51932, Sept. 8, 2008]

§211.86 Use of approved components, drug product containers, and closures.

Components, drug product containers, and closures approved for use shall be rotated so that the oldest approved stock is used first. Deviation from this requirement is permitted if such deviation is temporary and appropriate.

§211.87 Retesting of approved components, drug product containers, and closures.

Components, drug product containers, and closures shall be retested or reexamined, as appropriate, for identity, strength, quality, and purity and approved or rejected by the quality control unit in accordance with §211.84 as necessary, e.g., after storage for long periods or after exposure to air, heat or other conditions that might adversely affect the component, drug product container, or closure.

§211.89 Rejected components, drug product containers, and closures.

Rejected components, drug product containers, and closures shall be identified and controlled under a quarantine system designed to prevent their use in manufacturing or processing operations for which they are unsuitable.

§211.94 Drug product containers and closures.

(a) Drug product containers and closures shall not be reactive, additive, or absorptive so as to alter the safety, identity, strength, quality, or purity of the drug beyond the official or established requirements.

(b) Container closure systems shall provide adequate protection against foreseeable external factors in storage and use that can cause deterioration or contamination of the drug product.

(c) Drug product containers and closures shall be clean and, where indicated by the nature of the drug, sterilized and processed to remove pyrogenic properties to assure that they are suitable for their intended use. Such depyrogenation processes shall be validated.

(d) Standards or specifications, methods of testing, and, where indicated, methods of cleaning, sterilizing, and processing to remove pyrogenic properties shall be written and followed for drug product containers and closures.

(e) *Medical gas containers and closures must meet the following requirements*--(1) Gas-specific use outlet connections. Portable cryogenic medical gas containers that are not manufactured with permanent gas use outlet connections (*e.g.*, those that have been silver-brazed) must have gas-specific use outlet connections that are attached to the valve body so that they cannot be readily removed or replaced (without making the valve inoperable and preventing the containers' use) except by the manufacturer. For the purposes of this paragraph, the term "manufacturer" includes any individual or firm that fills high-pressure medical gas cylinders or cryogenic medical gas containers. For the purposes of this section, a "portable cryogenic medical gas container" is one that is capable of being transported and is intended to be attached to a medical gas supply system within a hospital, health care entity, nursing home, other facility, or home health care setting, or is a base unit used to fill small cryogenic gas containers for use by individual patients. The term does not include cryogenic containers that are not designed to be connected to a medical gas supply system, *e.g.*, tank trucks, trailers, rail cars, or small cryogenic gas containers for use by individual patients (including portable liquid oxygen units as defined at §868.5655 of this chapter).

(2) *Label and coloring requirements.* The labeling specified at §201.328(a) of this chapter must be affixed to the container in a manner that does not interfere with other labeling and such that it is not susceptible to becoming worn or inadvertently detached during normal use. Each such label as well as materials used for coloring medical gas containers must be reasonably resistant to fading, durable when exposed to atmospheric conditions, and not readily soluble in water.

[43 FR 45077, Sept. 29, 1978, as amended at 73 FR 51932, Sept. 8, 2008; 81 FR 81697, January 17, 2017]

Subpart F--Production and Process Controls

§211.100 Written procedures; deviations.

(a) There shall be written procedures for production and process control designed to assure that the drug products have the identity, strength, quality, and purity they purport or are represented to possess. Such procedures shall include all requirements in this subpart. These written procedures, including any changes, shall be drafted, reviewed, and approved by the appropriate organizational units and reviewed and approved by the quality control unit.

(b) Written production and process control procedures shall be followed in the execution of the various production and process control functions and shall be documented at the time of performance. Any deviation from the written procedures shall be recorded and justified.

§211.101 Charge-in of components.

Written production and control procedures shall include the following, which are designed to assure that the drug products produced have the identity, strength, quality, and purity they purport or are represented to possess:

(a) The batch shall be formulated with the intent to provide not less than 100 percent of the labeled or established amount of active ingredient.

(b) Components for drug product manufacturing shall be weighed, measured, or subdivided as appropriate. If a component is removed from the original container to another, the new container shall be identified with the following information:

(1) Component name or item code;
(2) Receiving or control number;
(3) Weight or measure in new container;
(4) Batch for which component was dispensed, including its product name, strength, and lot number.

(c) Weighing, measuring, or subdividing operations for components shall be adequately supervised. Each container of component dispensed to manufacturing shall be examined by a second person to assure that:

(1) The component was released by the quality control unit;
(2) The weight or measure is correct as stated in the batch production records;
(3) The containers are properly identified. If the weighing, measuring, or subdividing operations are performed by automated equipment under §211.68, only one person is needed to assure paragraphs (c)(1), (c)(2), and (c)(3) of this section.

(d) Each component shall either be added to the batch by one person and verified by a second person or, if the components are added by automated equipment under §211.68, only verified by one person.

[43 FR 45077, Sept. 29, 1978, as amended at 73 FR 51932, Sept. 8, 2008]

§211.103 Calculation of yield.

Actual yields and percentages of theoretical yield shall be determined at the conclusion of each appropriate phase of manufacturing, processing, packaging, or holding of the drug product. Such calculations shall either be performed by one person and independently verified by a second person, or, if the yield is calculated by automated equipment under § 211.68, be independently verified by one person.

[73 FR 51932, Sept. 8, 2008]

§211.105 Equipment identification.

(a) All compounding and storage containers, processing lines, and major equipment used during the production of a batch of a drug product shall be properly identified at all times to indicate their contents and, when necessary, the phase of processing of the batch.

(b) Major equipment shall be identified by a distinctive identification number or code that shall be recorded in the batch production record to show the specific equipment used in the manufacture of each batch of a drug product. In cases where only one of a particular type of equipment exists in a manufacturing facility, the name of the equipment may be used in lieu of a distinctive identification number or code.

§211.110 Sampling and testing of in-process materials and drug products.

(a) To assure batch uniformity and integrity of drug products, written procedures shall be established and followed that describe the in-process controls, and tests, or examinations to be conducted on appropriate samples of in-process materials of each batch. Such control procedures shall be established to monitor the output and to validate the performance of those manufacturing processes that may be responsible for causing variability in the characteristics of in-process material and the drug product. Such control procedures shall include, but are not limited to, the following, where appropriate:

(1) Tablet or capsule weight variation;
(2) Disintegration time;
(3) Adequacy of mixing to assure uniformity and homogeneity;
(4) Dissolution time and rate;
(5) Clarity, completeness, or pH of solutions.
(6) Bioburden testing.

(b) Valid in-process specifications for such characteristics shall be consistent with drug product final specifications and shall be derived from previous acceptable process average and process variability estimates where possible and determined by the application of suitable statistical procedures where appropriate. Examination and testing of samples shall assure that the drug product and in-process material conform to specifications.

(c) In-process materials shall be tested for identity, strength, quality, and purity as appropriate, and approved or rejected by the quality control unit, during the production process, e.g., at commencement or completion of significant phases or after storage for long periods.

(d) Rejected in-process materials shall be identified and controlled under a quarantine system designed to prevent their use in manufacturing or processing operations for which they are unsuitable.

[43 FR 45077, Sept. 29, 1978, as amended at 73 FR 51932, Sept. 8, 2008]

§211.111 Time limitations on production.

When appropriate, time limits for the completion of each phase of production shall be established to assure the quality of the drug product. Deviation from established time limits may be acceptable if such deviation does not compromise the quality of the drug product. Such deviation shall be justified and documented.

§211.113 Control of microbiological contamination.

(a) Appropriate written procedures, designed to prevent objectionable microorganisms in drug products not required to be sterile, shall be established and followed.

(b) Appropriate written procedures, designed to prevent microbiological contamination of drug products purporting to be sterile, shall be established and followed. Such procedures shall include validation of all aseptic and sterilization processes.

[43 FR 45077, Sept. 29, 1978, as amended at 73 FR 51932, Sept. 8, 2008]

§211.115   Reprocessing.

(a) Written procedures shall be established and followed prescribing a system for reprocessing batches that do not conform to standards or specifications and the steps to be taken to insure that the reprocessed batches will conform with all established standards, specifications, and characteristics.

(b) Reprocessing shall not be performed without the review and approval of the quality control unit.

Subpart G--Packaging and Labeling Control

§211.122   Materials examination and usage criteria.

(a) There shall be written procedures describing in sufficient detail the receipt, identification, storage, handling, sampling, examination, and/or testing of labeling and packaging materials; such written procedures shall be followed. Labeling and packaging materials shall be representatively sampled, and examined or tested upon receipt and before use in packaging or labeling of a drug product.

(b) Any labeling or packaging materials meeting appropriate written specifications may be approved and released for use. Any labeling or packaging materials that do not meet such specifications shall be rejected to prevent their use in operations for which they are unsuitable.

(c) Records shall be maintained for each shipment received of each different labeling and packaging material indicating receipt, examination or testing, and whether accepted or rejected.

(d) Labels and other labeling materials for each different drug product, strength, dosage form, or quantity of contents shall be stored separately with suitable identification. Access to the storage area shall be limited to authorized personnel.

(e) Obsolete and outdated labels, labeling, and other packaging materials shall be destroyed.

(f) Use of gang-printed labeling for different drug products, or different strengths or net contents of the same drug product, is prohibited unless the labeling from gang-printed sheets is adequately differentiated by size, shape, or color.

(g) If cut labeling is used for immediate container labels, individual unit cartons, or multiunit cartons containing immediate containers that are not packaged in individual unit cartons, packaging and labeling operations shall include one of the following special control procedures:

(1) Dedication of labeling and packaging lines to each different strength of each different drug product;

(2) Use of appropriate electronic or electromechanical equipment to conduct a 100-percent examination for correct labeling during or after completion of finishing operations; or

(3) Use of visual inspection to conduct a 100-percent examination for correct labeling during or after completion of finishing operations for hand-applied labeling. Such examination shall be performed by one person and independently verified by a second person.

(4) Use of any automated technique, including differentiation by labeling size and shape, that physically prevents incorrect labeling from being processed by labeling and packaging equipment.

(h) Printing devices on, or associated with, manufacturing lines used to imprint labeling upon the drug product unit label or case shall be monitored to assure that all imprinting conforms to the print specified in the batch production record.

[43 FR 45077, Sept. 29, 1978, as amended at 58 FR 41353, Aug. 3, 1993; 77 FR 16163, Mar. 20, 2012]

§211.125 Labeling issuance.

(a) Strict control shall be exercised over labeling issued for use in drug product labeling operations.

(b) Labeling materials issued for a batch shall be carefully examined for identity and conformity to the labeling specified in the master or batch production records.

(c) Procedures shall be used to reconcile the quantities of labeling issued, used, and returned, and shall require evaluation of discrepancies found between the quantity of drug product finished and the quantity of labeling issued when such discrepancies are outside narrow preset limits based on historical operating data. Such discrepancies shall be investigated in accordance with §211.192. Labeling reconciliation is waived for cut or roll labeling if a 100-percent examination for correct labeling is performed in accordance with §211.122(g)(2). Labeling reconciliation is also waived for 360° wraparound labels on portable cryogenic medical gas containers.

(d) All excess labeling bearing lot or control numbers shall be destroyed.

(e) Returned labeling shall be maintained and stored in a manner to prevent mixups and provide proper identification.

(f) Procedures shall be written describing in sufficient detail the control procedures employed for the issuance of labeling; such written procedures shall be followed.

[43 FR 45077, Sept. 29, 1978, as amended at 58 FR 41354, Aug. 3, 1993; 81 FR 81697, January 17, 2017]

§211.130 Packaging and labeling operations.

There shall be written procedures designed to assure that correct labels, labeling, and packaging materials are used for drug products; such written procedures shall be followed. These procedures shall incorporate the following features:

(a) Prevention of mixups and cross-contamination by physical or spatial separation from operations on other drug products.

(b) Identification and handling of filled drug product containers that are set aside and held in unlabeled condition for future labeling operations to preclude mislabeling of individual containers, lots, or portions of lots.

Identification need not be applied to each individual container but shall be sufficient to determine name, strength, quantity of contents, and lot or control number of each container.

(c) Identification of the drug product with a lot or control number that permits determination of the history of the manufacture and control of the batch.

(d) Examination of packaging and labeling materials for suitability and correctness before packaging operations, and documentation of such examination in the batch production record.

(e) Inspection of the packaging and labeling facilities immediately before use to assure that all drug products have been removed from previous operations. Inspection shall also be made to assure that packaging and labeling materials not suitable for subsequent operations have been removed. Results of inspection shall be documented in the batch production records.

[43 FR 45077, Sept. 29, 1978, as amended at 58 FR 41354, Aug. 3, 1993]

§211.132 Tamper-evident packaging requirements for over-the-counter (OTC) human drug products.

(a) *General.* The Food and Drug Administration has the authority under the Federal Food, Drug, and Cosmetic Act (the act) to establish a uniform national requirement for tamper-evident packaging of OTC drug products that will improve the security of OTC drug packaging and help assure the safety and effectiveness of OTC drug products. An OTC drug product (except a dermatological, dentifrice, insulin, or lozenge product) for retail sale that is not packaged in a tamper-resistant package or that is not properly labeled under this section is adulterated under section 501 of the act or misbranded under section 502 of the act, or both.

(b) *Requirements for tamper-evident package.* (1) Each manufacturer and packer who packages an OTC drug product (except a dermatological, dentifrice, insulin, or lozenge product) for retail sale shall package the product in a tamper-evident package, if this product is accessible to the public while held for sale. A tamper-evident package is one having one or more indicators or barriers to entry which, if breached or missing, can reasonably be expected to provide visible evidence to consumers that tampering has occurred. To reduce the likelihood of successful tampering and to increase the likelihood that consumers will discover if a product has been tampered with, the package is required to be distinctive by design or by the use of one or more indicators or barriers to entry that employ an identifying characteristic (e.g., a pattern, name, registered trademark, logo, or picture). For purposes of this section, the term "distinctive by design" means the packaging cannot be duplicated with commonly available materials or through commonly available processes. A tamper-evident package may involve an immediate-container and closure system or secondary-container or carton system or any combination of systems intended to provide a visual indication of package integrity. The tamper-evident feature shall be designed to and shall remain intact when handled in a reasonable manner during manufacture, distribution, and retail display.

(2) In addition to the tamper-evident packaging feature described in paragraph (b)(1) of this section, any two-piece, hard gelatin capsule covered by this section must be sealed using an acceptable tamper-evident technology.

(c) *Labeling.* (1) In order to alert consumers to the specific tamper-evident feature(s) used, each retail package of an OTC drug product covered by this section (except ammonia inhalant in crushable glass ampules, containers ofcompressed medical oxygen, or aerosol products that depend upon the power of a liquefied or compressed gas to expel the contents from the container) is required to bear a statement that:

(i) Identifies all tamper-evident feature(s) and any capsule sealing technologies used to comply with paragraph (b) of this section;

(ii) Is prominently placed on the package; and

(iii) Is so placed that it will be unaffected if the tamper-evident feature of the package is breached or missing.

(2) If the tamper-evident feature chosen to meet the requirements in paragraph (b) of this section uses an identifying characteristic, that characteristic is required to

be referred to in the labeling statement. For example, the labeling statement on a bottle with a shrink band could say "For your protection, this bottle has an imprinted seal around the neck."

(d) *Request for exemptions from packaging and labeling requirements*. A manufacturer or packer may request an exemption from the packaging and labeling requirements of this section. A request for an exemption is required to be submitted in the form of a citizen petition under §10.30 of this chapter and should be clearly identified on the envelope as a "Request for Exemption from the Tamper-Evident Packaging Rule." The petition is required to contain the following:

(1) The name of the drug product or, if the petition seeks an exemption for a drug class, the name of the drug class, and a list of products within that class.

(2) The reasons that the drug product's compliance with the tamper-evident packaging or labeling requirements of this section is unnecessary or cannot be achieved.

(3) A description of alternative steps that are available, or that the petitioner has already taken, to reduce the likelihood that the product or drug class will be the subject of malicious adulteration.

(4) Other information justifying an exemption.

(e) *OTC drug products subject to approved new drug applications*. Holders of approved new drug applications for OTC drug products are required under §314.70 of this chapter to provide the agency with notification of changes in packaging and labeling to comply with the requirements of this section. Changes in packaging and labeling required by this regulation may be made before FDA approval, as provided under §314.70(c) of this chapter. Manufacturing changes by which capsules are to be sealed require prior FDA approval under §314.70(b) of this chapter.

(f) *Poison Prevention Packaging Act of 1970*. This section does not affect any requirements for "special packaging" as defined under §310.3(l) of this chapter and required under the Poison Prevention Packaging Act of 1970. (Approved by the Office of Management and Budget under OMB control number 0910-0149)

[54 FR 5228, Feb. 2, 1989, as amended at 63 FR 59470, Nov. 4, 1998]

§211.134 Drug product inspection.

(a) Packaged and labeled products shall be examined during finishing operations to provide assurance that containers and packages in the lot have the correct label.

(b) A representative sample of units shall be collected at the completion of finishing operations and shall be visually examined for correct labeling.

(c) Results of these examinations shall be recorded in the batch production or control records.

§211.137 Expiration dating.

(a) To assure that a drug product meets applicable standards of identity, strength, quality, and purity at the time of use, it shall bear an expiration date determined by appropriate stability testing described in §211.166.

(b) Expiration dates shall be related to any storage conditions stated on the labeling, as determined by stability studies described in §211.166.

(c) If the drug product is to be reconstituted at the time of dispensing, its labeling shall bear expiration information for both the reconstituted and unreconstituted drug products.

(d) Expiration dates shall appear on labeling in accordance with the requirements of §201.17 of this chapter.

(e) Homeopathic drug products shall be exempt from the requirements of this section.

(f) Allergenic extracts that are labeled "No U.S. Standard of Potency" are exempt from the requirements of this section.

(g) New drug products for investigational use are exempt from the requirements of this section, provided that they meet appropriate standards or specifications as demonstrated by stability studies during their use in clinical investigations. Where new drug products for investigational use are to be reconstituted at the time of dispensing, their labeling shall bear expiration information for the reconstituted drug product.

(h) Pending consideration of a proposed exemption, published in the FEDERAL REGISTER of September 29,

1978, the requirements in this section shall not be enforced for human OTC drug products if their labeling does not bear dosage limitations and they are stable for at least 3 years as supported by appropriate stability data.

[43 FR 45077, Sept. 29, 1978, as amended at 46 FR 56412, Nov. 17, 1981; 60 FR 4091, Jan. 20, 1995]

Subpart H--Holding and Distribution

§211.142 Warehousing procedures.

Written procedures describing the warehousing of drug products shall be established and followed. They shall include:

(a) Quarantine of drug products before release by the quality control unit.

(b) Storage of drug products under appropriate conditions of temperature, humidity, and light so that the identity, strength, quality, and purity of the drug products are not affected.

§211.150 Distribution procedures.

Written procedures shall be established, and followed, describing the distribution of drug products. They shall include:

(a) A procedure whereby the oldest approved stock of a drug product is distributed first. Deviation from this requirement is permitted if such deviation is temporary and appropriate.

(b) A system by which the distribution of each lot of drug product can be readily determined to facilitate its recall if necessary.

Subpart I--Laboratory Controls

§211.160 General requirements.

(a) The establishment of any specifications, standards, sampling plans, test procedures, or other laboratory control mechanisms required by this subpart, including any change in such specifications, standards, sampling plans, test procedures, or other laboratory control mechanisms, shall be drafted by the appropriate organizational unit and reviewed and approved by the quality control unit. The requirements in this subpart shall be followed and shall be documented at the time of performance. Any deviation from the written specifications, standards, sampling plans, test procedures, or other laboratory control mechanisms shall be recorded and justified.

(b) Laboratory controls shall include the establishment of scientifically sound and appropriate specifications, standards, sampling plans, and test procedures designed to assure that components, drug product containers, closures, in-process materials, labeling, and drug products conform to appropriate standards of identity, strength, quality, and purity. Laboratory controls shall include:

(1) Determination of conformity to applicable written specifications for the acceptance of each lot within each shipment of components, drug product containers, closures, and labeling used in the manufacture, processing, packing, or holding of drug products. The specifications shall include a description of the sampling and testing procedures used. Samples shall be representative and adequately identified. Such procedures shall also require appropriate retesting of any component, drug product container, or closure that is subject to deterioration.

(2) Determination of conformance to written specifications and a description of sampling and testing procedures for in-process materials. Such samples shall be representative and properly identified.

(3) Determination of conformance to written descriptions of sampling procedures and appropriate specifications for drug products. Such samples shall be representative and properly identified.

(4) The calibration of instruments, apparatus, gauges, and recording devices at suitable intervals in accordance with an established written program containing specific directions, schedules, limits for accuracy and precision, and provisions for remedial action in the event accuracy and/or precision limits are not met. Instruments, apparatus, gauges, and recording devices not meeting established specifications shall not be used.

[43 FR 45077, Sept. 29, 1978, as amended at 73 FR 51932, Sept. 8, 2008]

§211.165 Testing and release for distribution.

(a) For each batch of drug product, there shall be appropriate laboratory determination of satisfactory conformance to final specifications for the drug product, including the identity and strength of each active ingredient, prior to release. Where sterility and/or pyrogen testing are conducted on specific batches of shortlived radiopharmaceuticals, such batches may be released prior to completion of sterility and/or pyrogen testing, provided such testing is completed as soon as possible.

(b) There shall be appropriate laboratory testing, as necessary, of each batch of drug product required to be free of objectionable microorganisms.

(c) Any sampling and testing plans shall be described in written procedures that shall include the method of sampling and the number of units per batch to be tested; such written procedure shall be followed.

(d) Acceptance criteria for the sampling and testing conducted by the quality control unit shall be adequate to assure that batches of drug products meet each appropriate specification and appropriate statistical quality control criteria as a condition for their approval and release. The statistical quality control criteria shall include appropriate acceptance levels and/or appropriate rejection levels.

(e) The accuracy, sensitivity, specificity, and reproducibility of test methods employed by the firm shall be established and documented. Such validation and documentation may be accomplished in accordance with §211.194(a)(2).

(f) Drug products failing to meet established standards or specifications and any other relevant quality control criteria shall be rejected. Reprocessing may be performed. Prior to acceptance and use, reprocessed material must meet appropriate standards, specifications, and any other relevant criteria.

§211.166 Stability testing.

(a) There shall be a written testing program designed to assess the stability characteristics of drug products. The results of such stability testing shall be used in determining appropriate storage conditions and expiration dates. The written program shall be followed and shall include:

(1) Sample size and test intervals based on statistical criteria for each attribute examined to assure valid estimates of stability;

(2) Storage conditions for samples retained for testing;

(3) Reliable, meaningful, and specific test methods;

(4) Testing of the drug product in the same container-closure system as that in which the drug product is marketed;

(5) Testing of drug products for reconstitution at the time of dispensing (as directed in the labeling) as well as after they are reconstituted.

(b) An adequate number of batches of each drug product shall be tested to determine an appropriate expiration date and a record of such data shall be maintained. Accelerated studies, combined with basic stability information on the components, drug products, and container-closure system, may be used to support tentative expiration dates provided full shelf life studies are not available and are being conducted. Where data from accelerated studies are used to project a tentative expiration date that is beyond a date supported by actual shelf life studies, there must be stability studies conducted, including drug product testing at appropriate intervals, until the tentative expiration date is verified or the appropriate expiration date determined.

(c) For homeopathic drug products, the requirements of this section are as follows:

(1) There shall be a written assessment of stability based at least on testing or examination of the drug product for compatibility of the ingredients, and based on marketing experience with the drug product to indicate that there is no degradation of the product for the normal or expected period of use.

(2) Evaluation of stability shall be based on the same container-closure system in which the drug product is being marketed.

(d) Allergenic extracts that are labeled "No U.S. Standard of Potency" are exempt from the requirements of this section.

[43 FR 45077, Sept. 29, 1978, as amended at 46 FR 56412, Nov. 17, 1981]

§211.167 Special testing requirements.

(a) For each batch of drug product purporting to be sterile and/or pyrogen-free, there shall be appropriate laboratory testing to determine conformance to such requirements. The test procedures shall be in writing and shall be followed.

(b) For each batch of ophthalmic ointment, there shall be appropriate testing to determine conformance to specifications regarding the presence of foreign particles and harsh or abrasive substances. The test procedures shall be in writing and shall be followed.

(c) For each batch of controlled-release dosage form, there shall be appropriate laboratory testing to determine conformance to the specifications for the rate of release of each active ingredient. The test procedures shall be in writing and shall be followed.

§211.170 Reserve samples.

(a) An appropriately identified reserve sample that is representative of each lot in each shipment of each active ingredient shall be retained. The reserve sample consists of at least twice the quantity necessary for all tests required to determine whether the active ingredient meets its established specifications, except for sterility and pyrogen testing. The retention time is as follows:

(1) For an active ingredient in a drug product other than those described in paragraphs (a) (2) and (3) of this section, the reserve sample shall be retained for 1 year after the expiration date of the last lot of the drug product containing the active ingredient.

(2) For an active ingredient in a radioactive drug product, except for nonradioactive reagent kits, the reserve sample shall be retained for:

(i) Three months after the expiration date of the last lot of the drug product containing the active ingredient if the expiration dating period of the drug product is 30 days or less; or

(ii) Six months after the expiration date of the last lot of the drug product containing the active ingredient if the expiration dating period of the drug product is more than 30 days.

(3) For an active ingredient in an OTC drug product that is exempt from bearing an expiration date under §211.137, the reserve sample shall be retained for 3 years after distribution of the last lot of the drug product containing the active ingredient.

(b) An appropriately identified reserve sample that is representative of each lot or batch of drug product shall be retained and stored under conditions consistent with product labeling. The reserve sample shall be stored in the same immediate container-closure system in which the drug product is marketed or in one that has essentially the same characteristics. The reserve sample consists of at least twice the quantity necessary to perform all the required tests, except those for sterility and pyrogens. Except for those for drug products described in paragraph (b)(2) of this section, reserve samples from representative sample lots or batches selected by acceptable statistical procedures shall be examined visually at least once a year for evidence of deterioration unless visual examination would affect the integrity of the reserve sample. Any evidence of reserve sample deterioration shall be investigated in accordance with §211.192. The results of the examination shall be recorded and maintained with other stability data on the drug product. Reserve samples of compressed medical gases need not be retained. The retention time is as follows:

(1) For a drug product other than those described in paragraphs (b) (2) and (3) of this section, the reserve sample shall be retained for 1 year after the expiration date of the drug product.

(2) For a radioactive drug product, except for nonradioactive reagent kits, the reserve sample shall be retained for:

(i) Three months after the expiration date of the drug product if the expiration dating period of the drug product is 30 days or less; or

(ii) Six months after the expiration date of the drug product if the expiration dating period of the drug product is more than 30 days.

(3) For an OTC drug product that is exempt for bearing an expiration date under §211.137, the reserve sample must be retained for 3 years after the lot or batch of drug product is distributed.

[48 FR 13025, Mar. 29, 1983, as amended at 60 FR 4091, Jan. 20, 1995]

§211.173   Laboratory animals.

Animals used in testing components, in-process materials, or drug products for compliance with established specifications shall be maintained and controlled in a manner that assures their suitability for their intended use. They shall be identified, and adequate records shall be maintained showing the history of their use.

§211.176   Penicillin contamination.

If a reasonable possibility exists that a non-penicillin drug product has been exposed to cross-contamination with penicillin, the non-penicillin drug product shall be tested for the presence of penicillin. Such drug product shall not be marketed if detectable levels are found when tested according to procedures specified in 'Procedures for Detecting and Measuring Penicillin Contamination in Drugs,' which is incorporated by reference. Copies are available from the Division of Research and Testing (HFD-470), Center for Drug Evaluation and Research, Food and Drug Administration, 5001 Campus Dr.., College Park, MD 20740, or available for inspection at the National Archives and Records Administration (NARA). For information onthe availability of this material at NARA, call 202-741-6030, or go to:
http://www.archives.gov/federal_register/code_of_feder al_regulations/ibr_locations.html.

[43 FR 45077, Sept. 29, 1978, as amended at 47 FR 9396, Mar. 5, 1982; 50 FR 8996, Mar. 6, 1985; 55 FR 11577, Mar. 29, 1990; 66 FR 56035, Nov. 6, 2001; 69 FR 18803, Apr. 9, 2004; 81 FR 49897, July 29, 2016]

Subpart J--Records and Reports

§211.180 General requirements.

(a) Any production, control, or distribution record that is required to be maintained in compliance with this part and is specifically associated with a batch of a drug product shall be retained for at least 1 year after the expiration date of the batch or, in the case of certain OTC drug products lacking expiration dating because they meet the criteria for exemption under §211.137, 3 years after distribution of the batch.

(b) Records shall be maintained for all components, drug product containers, closures, and labeling for at least 1 year after the expiration date or, in the case of certain OTC drug products lacking expiration dating because they meet the criteria for exemption under §211.137, 3 years after distribution of the last lot of drug product incorporating the component or using the container, closure, or labeling.

(c) All records required under this part, or copies of such records, shall be readily available for authorized inspection during the retention period at the establishment where the activities described in such records occurred. These records or copies thereof shall be subject to photocopying or other means of reproduction as part of such inspection. Records that can be immediately retrieved from another location by computer or other electronic means shall be considered as meeting the requirements of this paragraph.

(d) Records required under this part may be retained either as original records or as true copies such as photocopies, microfilm, microfiche, or other accurate reproductions of the original records. Where reduction techniques, such as microfilming, are used, suitable reader and photocopying equipment shall be readily available.

(e) Written records required by this part shall be maintained so that data therein can be used for evaluating, at least annually, the quality standards of each drug product to determine the need for changes in drug product specifications or manufacturing or control procedures. Written procedures shall be established and followed for such evaluations and shall include provisions for:

(1) A review of a representative number of batches, whether approved or rejected, and, where applicable, records associated with the batch.

(2) A review of complaints, recalls, returned or salvaged drug products, and investigations conducted under §211.192 for each drug product.

(f) Procedures shall be established to assure that the responsible officials of the firm, if they are not personally involved in or immediately aware of such actions, are notified in writing of any investigations conducted under §§211.198, 211.204, or 211.208 of these regulations, any recalls, reports of inspectional observations issued by the Food and Drug Administration, or any regulatory actions relating to good manufacturing practices brought by the Food and Drug Administration.

[43 FR 45077, Sept. 29, 1978, as amended at 60 FR 4091, Jan. 20, 1995]

§211.182 Equipment cleaning and use log.

A written record of major equipment cleaning, maintenance (except routine maintenance such as lubrication and adjustments), and use shall be included in individual equipment logs that show the date, time, product, and lot number of each batch processed. If equipment is dedicated to manufacture of one product, then individual equipment logs are not required, provided that lots or batches of such product follow in numerical order and are manufactured in numerical sequence. In cases where dedicated equipment is employed, the records of cleaning, maintenance, and use shall be part of the batch record. The persons performing and double-checking the cleaning and maintenance (or, if the cleaning and maintenance is performed using automated equipment under §211.68, just the person verifying the cleaning and maintenance done by the automated equipment) shall date and sign or initial the log indicating that the work was performed. Entries in the log shall be in chronological order.

§211.184 Component, drug product container, closure, and labeling records.

These records shall include the following:

(a) The identity and quantity of each shipment of each lot of components, drug product containers, closures, and labeling; the name of the supplier; the supplier's lot number(s) if known; the receiving code as specified in §211.80; and the date of receipt. The name and location of the prime manufacturer, if different from the supplier, shall be listed if known.

(b) The results of any test or examination performed (including those performed as required by §211.82(a), §211.84(d), or §211.122(a)) and the conclusions derived therefrom.

(c) An individual inventory record of each component, drug product container, and closure and, for each component, a reconciliation of the use of each lot of such component. The inventory record shall contain sufficient information to allow determination of any batch or lot of drug product associated with the use of each component, drug product container, and closure.

(d) Documentation of the examination and review of labels and labeling for conformity with established specifications in accord with §§211.122(c) and 211.130(c).

(e) The disposition of rejected components, drug product containers, closure, and labeling.

§211.186 Master production and control records.

(a) To assure uniformity from batch to batch, master production and control records for each drug product, including each batch size thereof, shall be prepared, dated, and signed (full signature, handwritten) by one person and independently checked, dated, and signed by a second person. The preparation of master production and control records shall be described in a written procedure and such written procedure shall be followed.

(b) Master production and control records shall include:

(1) The name and strength of the product and a description of the dosage form;

(2) The name and weight or measure of each active ingredient per dosage unit or per unit of weight or measure of the drug product, and a statement of the total weight or measure of any dosage unit;

(3) A complete list of components designated by names or codes sufficiently specific to indicate any special quality characteristic;

(4) An accurate statement of the weight or measure of each component, using the same weight system (metric, avoirdupois, or apothecary) for each component. Reasonable variations may be permitted, however, in the amount of components necessary for the preparation in the dosage form, provided they are justified in the master production and control records;

(5) A statement concerning any calculated excess of component;

(6) A statement of theoretical weight or measure at appropriate phases of processing;

(7) A statement of theoretical yield, including the maximum and minimum percentages of theoretical yield beyond which investigation according to §211.192 is required;

(8) A description of the drug product containers, closures, and packaging materials, including a specimen or copy of each label and all other labeling signed and dated by the person or persons responsible for approval of such labeling;

(9) Complete manufacturing and control instructions, sampling and testing procedures, specifications, special notations, and precautions to be followed.

§211.188 Batch production and control records.

Batch production and control records shall be prepared for each batch of drug product produced and shall include complete information relating to the production and control of each batch. These records shall include:

(a) An accurate reproduction of the appropriate master production or control record, checked for accuracy, dated, and signed;

(b) Documentation that each significant step in the manufacture, processing, packing, or holding of the batch was accomplished, including:

(1) Dates;

(2) Identity of individual major equipment and lines used;

(3) Specific identification of each batch of component or in-process material used;

(4) Weights and measures of components used in the course of processing;

(5) In-process and laboratory control results;

(6) Inspection of the packaging and labeling area before and after use;

(7) A statement of the actual yield and a statement of the percentage of theoretical yield at appropriate phases of processing;

(8) Complete labeling control records, including specimens or copies of all labeling used;

(9) Description of drug product containers and closures;

(10) Any sampling performed;

(11) Identification of the persons performing and directly supervising or checking each significant step in the operation, or if a significant step in the operation is performed by automated equipment under §211.68, the identification of the person checking the significant step performed by the automated equipment.

(12) Any investigation made according to §211.192.

(13) Results of examinations made in accordance with §211.134.

[43 FR 45077, Sept. 29, 1978, as amended at 73 FR 51933, Sept. 8, 2008]

§211.192 Production record review.

All drug product production and control records, including those for packaging and labeling, shall be reviewed and approved by the quality control unit to determine compliance with all established, approved written procedures before a batch is released or distributed. Any unexplained discrepancy (including a percentage of theoretical yield exceeding the maximum or minimum percentages established in master production and control records) or the failure of a batch or any of its components to meet any of its specifications shall be thoroughly investigated, whether or not the batch has already been distributed. The investigation shall extend to other batches of the same drug product and other drug products that may have been associated with the specific failure or discrepancy. A written record of the investigation shall be made and shall include the conclusions and follow up.

§211.194 Laboratory records.

(a) Laboratory records shall include complete data derived from all tests necessary to assure compliance with established specifications and standards, including examinations and assays, as follows:

(1) A description of the sample received for testing with identification of source (that is, location from where sample was obtained), quantity, lot number or other distinctive code, date sample was taken, and date sample was received for testing.

(2) A statement of each method used in the testing of the sample. The statement shall indicate the location of data that establish that the methods used in the testing of the sample meet proper standards of accuracy and reliability as applied to the product tested. (If the method employed is in the current revision of the United States Pharmacopeia, National Formulary, AOAC INTERNATIONAL, Book of Methods,[1] or in other recognized standard references, or is detailed in an approved new drug application and the referenced method is not modified, a statement indicating the method and reference will suffice). The suitability of all testing methods used shall be verified under actual conditions of use.

(3) A statement of the weight or measure of sample used for each test, where appropriate.

(4) A complete record of all data secured in the course of each test, including all graphs, charts, and spectra from laboratory instrumentation, properly identified to show the specific component, drug product container, closure, in-process material, or drug product, and lot tested.

---

[1]Copies may be obtained from: AOAC INTERNATIONAL, 481 North Frederick Ave., suite 500, Gaithersburg, MD 20877

(5) A record of all calculations performed in connection with the test, including units of measure, conversion factors, and equivalency factors.

(6) A statement of the results of tests and how the results compare with established standards of identity, strength, quality, and purity for the component, drug productcontainer, closure, in-process material, or drug product tested.

(7) The initials or signature of the person who performs each test and the date(s) the tests were performed.

(8) The initials or signature of a second person showing that the original records have been reviewed for accuracy, completeness, and compliance with established standards.

(b) Complete records shall be maintained of any modification of an established method employed in testing. Such records shall include the reason for the modification and data to verify that the modification produced results that are at least as accurate and reliable for the material being tested as the established method.

(c) Complete records shall be maintained of any testing and standardization of laboratory reference standards, reagents, and standard solutions.

(d) Complete records shall be maintained of the periodic calibration of laboratory instruments, apparatus, gauges, and recording devices required by §211.160(b)(4).

(e) Complete records shall be maintained of all stability testing performed in accordance with §211.166.

[43 FR 45077, Sept. 29, 1978, as amended at 55 FR 11577, Mar. 29, 1990; 65 FR 18889, Apr. 10, 2000; 70 FR 40880, July 15, 2005; 70 FR 67651, Nov. 8, 2005]

§211.196 Distribution records.

Distribution records shall contain the name and strength of the product and description of the dosage form, name and address of the consignee, date and quantity shipped, and lot or control number of the drug product. For compressed medical gas products, distribution records are not required to contain lot or control numbers.

(Approved by the Office of Management and Budget under control number 0910-0139) [49 FR 9865, Mar. 16, 1984]

§211.198 Complaint files.

(a) Written procedures describing the handling of all written and oral complaints regarding a drug product shall be established and followed. Such procedures shall include provisions for review by the quality control unit, of any complaint involving the possible failure of a drug product to meet any of its specifications and, for such drug products, a determination as to the need for an investigation in accordance with §211.192. Such procedures shall include provisions for review to determine whether the complaint represents a serious and unexpected adverse drug experience which is required to be reported to the Food and Drug Administration in accordance with §§310.305 and 514.80 of this chapter.

(b) A written record of each complaint shall be maintained in a file designated for drug product complaints. The file regarding such drug product complaints shall be maintained at the establishment where the drug product involved was manufactured, processed, or packed, or such file may be maintained at another facility if the written records in such files are readily available for inspection at that other facility. Written records involving a drug product shall be maintained until at least 1 year after the expiration date of the drug product, or 1 year after the date that the complaint was received, whichever is longer. In the case of certain OTC drug products lacking expiration dating because they meet the criteria for exemption under §211.137, such written records shall be maintained for 3 years after distribution of the drug product.

(1) The written record shall include the following information, where known: the name and strength of the drug product, lot number, name of complainant, nature of complaint, and reply to complainant.

(2) Where an investigation under §211.192 is conducted, the written record shall include the findings of the investigation and follow up. The record or copy of the record of the investigation shall be maintained at the establishment where the investigation occurred in accordance with §211.180(c).

(3) Where an investigation under §211.192 is not conducted, the written record shall include the reason that an investigation was found not to be necessary and the name of the responsible person making such a determination.

[43 FR 45077, Sept. 29, 1978, as amended at 51 FR 24479, July 3, 1986; 68 FR 15364, Mar. 31, 2003]

Subpart K--Returned and Salvaged Drug Products

§211.204 Returned drug products.

Returned drug products shall be identified as such and held. If the conditions under which returned drug products have been held, stored, or shipped before or during their return, or if the condition of the drug product, its container, carton, or labeling, as a result of storage or shipping, casts doubt on the safety, identity, strength, quality or purity of the drug product, the returned drug product shall be destroyed unless examination, testing, or other investigations prove the drug product meets appropriate standards of safety, identity, strength, quality, or purity. A drug product may be reprocessed provided the subsequent drug product meets appropriate standards, specifications, and characteristics. Records of returned drug products shall be maintained and shall include the name and label potency of the drug product dosage form, lot number (or control number or batch number), reason for the return, quantity returned, date of disposition, and ultimate disposition of the returned drug product. If the reason for a drug product being returned implicates associated batches, an appropriate investigation shall be conducted in accordance with the requirements of §211.192. Procedures for the holding, testing, and reprocessing of returned drug products shall be in writing and shall be followed.

§211.208 Drug product salvaging.

Drug products that have been subjected to improper storage conditions including extremes in temperature, humidity, smoke, fumes, pressure, age, or radiation due to natural disasters, fires, accidents, or equipment failures shall not be salvaged and returned to the marketplace. Whenever there is a question whether drug products have been subjected to such conditions, salvaging operations may be conducted only if there is (a) evidence from laboratory tests and assays (including animal feeding studies where applicable) that the drug products meet all applicable standards of identity, strength, quality, and purity and (b) evidence from inspection of the premises that the drug products and their associated packaging were not subjected to improper storage conditions as a result of the disaster or accident. Organoleptic examinations shall be acceptable only as supplemental evidence that the drug products meet appropriate standards of identity, strength, quality, and purity. Records including name, lot number, and disposition shall be maintained for drug products subject to this section.

Notes

Part 820

The Code of Federal Regulations
Title 21 – Food and Drugs

Part 820
QUALITY SYSTEM REGULATION

Printed by GMP Publications, Inc.
Tel: 866-544-9007 or 856-810-7331
Fax: 866-544-9002
http://www.gmppublications.com
sales@gmppublications.com

PART 820--QUALITY SYSTEM REGULATION

Subpart A--General Provisions

§820.1 Scope.
§820.3 Definitions.
§820.5 Quality system.

Subpart B--Quality System Requirements

§820.20 Management responsibility.
§820.22 Quality audit.
§820.25 Personnel.

Subpart C--Design Controls

§820.30 Design controls.

Subpart D--Document Controls

§820.40 Document controls.

Subpart E--Purchasing Controls

§820.50 Purchasing controls.

Subpart F--Identification and Traceability

§820.60 Identification.
§820.65 Traceability.

Subpart G--Production and Process Controls

§820.70 Production and process controls.
§820.72 Inspection, measuring, and test equipment.
§820.75 Process validation.

Subpart H--Acceptance Activities

§820.80 Receiving, in-process, and finished device acceptance.
§820.86 Acceptance status.

Subpart I--Nonconforming Product

§820.90 Nonconforming product.

Subpart J--Corrective and Preventive Action

§820.100 Corrective and preventive action.

Subpart K--Labeling and Packaging Control

§820.120 Device labeling.
§820.130 Device packaging.

Subpart L--Handling, Storage, Distribution, and Installation

§820.140 Handling.
§820.150 Storage.
§820.160 Distribution.
§820.170 Installation.

Subpart M--Records

§820.180 General requirements.
§820.181 Device master record.
§820.184 Device history record.
§820.186 Quality system record.
§820.198 Complaint files.

Subpart N--Servicing

§820.200 Servicing.

Subpart O--Statistical Techniques

§820.250 Statistical techniques.

Authority: 21 U.S.C. 351, 352, 360, 360c, 360d, 360e, 360h, 360i, 360j, 360l, 371, 374, 381, 383; 42 U.S.C. 216, 262, 263a, 264.

Source: 61 FR 52654, Oct. 7, 1996, unless otherwise noted.

21 CFR PART 820
QUALITY SYSTEM REGULATION

Subpart A--General Provisions

§820.1 Scope.

(a) *Applicability.*

(1) Current good manufacturing practice (CGMP) requirements are set forth in this quality system regulation. The requirements in this part govern the methods used in, and the facilities and controls used for, the design, manufacture, packaging, labeling, storage, installation, and servicing of all finished devices intended for human use. The requirements in this part are intended to ensure that finished devices will be safe and effective and otherwise in compliance with the Federal Food, Drug, and Cosmetic Act (the act). This part establishes basic requirements applicable to manufacturers of finished medical devices. If a manufacturer engages in only some operations subject to the requirements in this part, and not in others, that manufacturer need only comply with those requirements applicable to the operations in which it is engaged. With respect to class I devices, design controls apply only to those devices listed in §820.30(a)(2). This regulation does not apply to manufacturers of components or parts of finished devices, but such manufacturers are encouraged to use appropriate provisions of this regulation as guidance. Manufacturers of blood and blood components used for transfusion or for further manufacturing are not subject to this part, but are subject to subchapter F of this chapter. Manufacturers of human cells, tissues, and cellular and tissue-based products (HCT/Ps), as defined in §1271.3(d) of this chapter, that are medical devices (subject to premarket review or notification, or exempt from notification, under an application submitted under the device provisions of the act or under a biological product license application under sec-

tion 351 of the Public Health Service Act) are subject to this part and are also subject to the donor-eligibility procedures set forth in part 1271 subpart C of this chapter and applicable current good tissue practice procedures in part 1271 subpart D of this chapter. In the event of a conflict between applicable regulations in part 1271 and in other parts of this chapter, the regulation specifically applicable to the device in question shall supersede the more general.

(2) The provisions of this part shall be applicable to any finished device as defined in this part, intended for human use, that is manufactured, imported, or offered for import in any State or Territory of the United States, the District of Columbia, or the Commonwealth of Puerto Rico.

(3) In this regulation the term "where appropriate" is used several times. When a requirement is qualified by "where appropriate," it is deemed to be "appropriate"unless the manufacturer can document justification otherwise. A requirement is "appropriate" if nonimplementation could reasonably be expected to result in the product not meeting its specified requirements or the manufacturer not being able to carry out any necessary corrective action.

(b) The quality system regulation in this part supplements regulations in other parts of this chapter except where explicitly stated otherwise. In the event of a conflict between applicable regulations in this part and in other parts of this chapter, the regulations specifically applicable to the device in question shall supersede any other generally applicable requirements.

(c) *Authority.* Part 820 is established and issued under authority of sections 501, 502, 510, 513, 514, 515, 518, 519, 520, 522, 701, 704, 801, 803 of the act (21 U.S.C. 351, 352, 360, 360c, 360d, 360e, 360h, 360i, 360j, 360l, 371, 374, 381, 383). The failure to comply with any applicable provision in this part renders a device adulterated under section 501(h) of the act. Such a device, as well as any person responsible for the failure to comply, is subject to regulatory action.

(d) *Foreign manufacturers.* If a manufacturer who offers devices for import into the United States refuses to permit or allow the completion of a Food and Drug Administration (FDA) inspection of the foreign facility for the purpose of determining compliance with this part, it shall appear for purposes of section 801(a) of the act, that the methods used in, and the facilities and controls used for, the design, manufacture, packaging, labeling, storage, installation, or servicing of any devices produced at such facility that are offered for import into the United States do not conform to the requirements of section 520(f) of the act and this part and that the devices manufactured at that facility are adulterated under section 501(h) of the act.

(e) *Exemptions or variances.*

(1) Any person who wishes to petition for an exemption or variance from any device quality system requirement is subject to the requirements of section 520(f)(2) of the act. Petitions for an exemption or variance shall be submitted according to the procedures set forth in Sec. 10.30 of this chapter, the FDA's administrative procedures. Guidance is available from the Center for Devices and Radiological Health, Division of Small Manufacturers, International and Consumer Assistance 10903 New Hampshire Ave., Bldg. 66, rm. 4613, Silver Spring, MD 20993-0002, 1-800-638-2041 or 301-796-7100, FAX: 301-847-8149.

(2) FDA may initiate and grant a variance from any device quality system requirement when the agency determines that such variance is in the best interest of the public health. Such variance will remain in effect only so long as there remains a public health need for the device and the device would not likely be made sufficiently available without the variance.

[61 FR 52654, Oct. 7, 1996, as amended at 65 FR 17136, Mar. 31, 2000; 65 FR 66636, Nov. 7, 2000; 69 FR 29829, May 25, 2005; 72 FR 17399, Apr. 9, 2007; 75 FR 20915, Apr. 22, 2010; 80 FR 29906, May 22, 2015]

§820.3 Definitions.

(a) *Act* means the Federal Food, Drug, and Cosmetic Act, as amended (secs. 201-903, 52 Stat. 1040 et seq., as amended (21 U.S.C. 321-394)). All definitions in section 201 of the act shall apply to the regulations in this part.

(b) *Complaint* means any written, electronic, or oral communication that alleges deficiencies related to the identity, quality, durability, reliability, safety, effectiveness, or performance of a device after it is released for distribution.

(c) *Component* means any raw material, substance, piece, part, software, firmware, labeling, or assembly which is intended to be included as part of the finished, packaged, and labeled device.

(d) *Control number* means any distinctive symbols, such as a distinctive combination of letters or numbers, or both, from which the history of the manufacturing, packaging, labeling, and distribution of a unit, lot, or batch of finished devices can be determined.

(e) *Design history file (DHF)* means a compilation of records which describes the design history of a finished device.

(f) *Design input* means the physical and performance requirements of a device that are used as a basis for device design.

(g) *Design output* means the results of a design effort at each design phase and at the end of the total design effort. The finished design output is the basis for the device master record. The total finished design output consists of the device, its packaging and labeling, and the device master record.

(h) *Design review* means a documented, comprehensive, systematic examination of a design to evaluate the adequacy of the design requirements, to evaluate the capability of the design to meet these requirements, and to identify problems.

(i) *Device history record (DHR)* means a compilation of records containing the production history of a finished device.

(j) *Device master record (DMR)* means a compilation of records containing the procedures and specifications for a finished device.

(k) *Establish* means define, document (in writing or electronically), and implement.

(l) *Finished device* means any device or accessory to any device that is suitable for use or capable of functioning, whether or not it is packaged, labeled, or sterilized.

(m) *Lot or batch* means one or more components or finished devices that consist of a single type, model, class, size, composition, or software version that are manufactured under essentially the same conditions and that are intended to have uniform characteristics and quality within specified limits.

(n) *Management with executive responsibility* means those senior employees of a manufacturer who have the authority to establish or make changes to the manufacturer's quality policy and quality system.

(o) *Manufacturer* means any person who designs, manufactures, fabricates, assembles, or processes a finished device. Manufacturer includes but is not limited to those who perform the functions of contract sterilization, installation, relabeling, remanufacturing, repacking, or specification development, and initial distributors of foreign entities performing these functions.

(p) *Manufacturing material* means any material or substance used in or used to facilitate the manufacturing process, a concomitant constituent, or a byproduct constituent produced during the manufacturing process, which is present in or on the finished device as a residue or impurity not by design or intent of the manufacturer.

(q) *Nonconformity* means the nonfulfillment of a specified requirement.

(r) *Product* means components, manufacturing materials, in-process devices, finished devices, and returned devices.

(s) *Quality* means the totality of features and characteristics that bear on the ability of a device to satisfy fitness-for-use, including safety and performance.

(t) *Quality audit* means a systematic, independent examination of a manufacturer's quality system that is performed at defined intervals and at sufficient frequency to determine whether both quality system activities and the results of such activities comply with quality system procedures, that these procedures are implemented effectively, and that these procedures are suitable to achieve quality system objectives.

(u) *Quality policy* means the overall intentions and direction of an organization with respect to quality, as established by management with executive responsibility.

(v) *Quality system* means the organizational structure, responsibilities, procedures, processes, and resources for implementing quality management.

(w) *Remanufacturer* means any person who processes, conditions, renovates, repackages, restores, or does any other act to a finished device that significantly changes the finished device's performance or safety specifications, or intended use.

(x) *Rework* means action taken on a nonconforming product so that it will fulfill the specified DMR requirements before it is released for distribution.

(y) *Specification* means any requirement with which a product, process, service, or other activity must conform.

(z) *Validation* means confirmation by examination and provision of objective evidence that the particular requirements for a specific intended use can be consistently fulfilled.

(1) *Process validation* means establishing by objective evidence that a process consistently produces a result or product meeting its predetermined specifications.

(2) *Design validation* means establishing by objective evidence that device specifications conform with user needs and intended use(s).

(aa) *Verification* means confirmation by examination and provision of objective evidence that specified requirements have been fulfilled.

(bb) *Human cell, tissue, or cellular or tissue-based product (HCT/P) regulated as a device* means an HCT/P as defined in §1271.3(d) of this chapter that does not meet the criteria in §1271.10(a) and that is also regulated as a device.

(cc) *Unique device identifier (UDI)* means an identifier that adequately identifies a device through its distribution and use by meeting the requirements of §830.20 of this chapter. A unique device identifier is composed of:

(1) A *device identifier* - a mandatory, fixed portion of a UDI that identifies the specific version or model of a device and the labeler of that device; and

(2) A *production identifier* - a conditional, variable portion of a UDI that identifies one or more of the following when included on the label of the device:

(i) The lot or batch within which a device was manufactured;

(ii) The serial number of a specific device;

(iii) The expiration date of a specific device;

(iv) The date a specific device was manufactured.

(v) For an HCT/P regulated as a device, the distinct identification code required by §1271.290(c) of this chapter.

(dd) *Universal product code (UPC)* means the product identifier used to identify an item sold at retail in the United States.

[61 FR 52654, Oct. 7, 1996, as amended at 78 FR 55822, Sept. 24, 2013]

§820.5   Quality system.

Each manufacturer shall establish and maintain a quality system that is appropriate for the specific medical device(s) designed or manufactured, and that meets the requirements of this part.

Subpart B--Quality System Requirements

§820.20   Management responsibility.

(a) *Quality policy.* Management with executive responsibility shall establish its policy and objectives for, and commitment to, quality. Management with executive responsibility shall ensure that the quality policy is understood, implemented, and maintained at all levels of the organization.

(b) *Organization.* Each manufacturer shall establish and maintain an adequate organizational structure to ensure that devices are designed and produced in accordance with the requirements of this part.

(1) *Responsibility and authority.* Each manufacturer shall establish the appropriate responsibility, authority, and interrelation of all personnel who manage, perform, and assess work affecting quality, and provide the independence and authority necessary to perform these tasks.

(2) *Resources.* Each manufacturer shall provide adequate resources, including the assignment of trained personnel, for management, performance of work, and assessment activities, including internal quality audits, to meet the requirements of this part.

(3) *Management representative.* Management with executive responsibility shall appoint, and document such appointment of, a member of management who, irrespective of other responsibilities, shall have established authority over and responsibility for:

(i) Ensuring that quality system requirements are effectively established and effectively maintained in accordance with this part; and

(ii) Reporting on the performance of the quality system to management with executive responsibility for review.

(c) *Management review.* Management with executive responsibility shall review the suitability and effectiveness of the quality system at defined intervals and with sufficient frequency according to established procedures to ensure that the quality system satisfies the requirements of this part and the manufacturer's established quality policy and objectives. The dates and results of quality system reviews shall be documented.

(d) *Quality planning.* Each manufacturer shall establish a quality plan which defines the quality practices, resources, and activities relevant to devices that are designed and manufactured. The manufacturer shall establish how the requirements for quality will be met.

(e) *Quality system procedures.* Each manufacturer shall establish quality system procedures and instructions. An outline of the structure of the documentation used in the quality system shall be established where appropriate.

§820.22 Quality audit.

Each manufacturer shall establish procedures for quality audits and conduct such audits to assure that the quality system is in compliance with the established quality system requirements and to determine the effectiveness of the quality system. Quality audits shall be conducted by individuals who do not have direct responsibility for the matters being audited. Corrective action(s), including a reaudit of deficient matters, shall be taken when necessary. A report of the results of each quality audit, and reaudit(s) where taken, shall be made and such reports shall be reviewed by management having responsibility for the matters audited. The dates and results of quality audits and reaudits shall be documented.

§820.25 Personnel.

(a) General. Each manufacturer shall have sufficient personnel with the necessary education, background, training, and experience to assure that all activities required by this part are correctly performed.

(b) Training. Each manufacturer shall establish procedures for identifying training needs and ensure that all personnel are trained to adequately perform their assigned responsibilities. Training shall be documented.

(1) As part of their training, personnel shall be made aware of device defects which may occur from the improper performance of their specific jobs.

(2) Personnel who perform verification and validation activities shall be made aware of defects and errors that may be encountered as part of their job functions.

Subpart C--Design Controls

§820.30 Design controls.

(a) *General.*

(1) Each manufacturer of any class III or class II device, and the class I devices listed in paragraph (a)(2) of this section, shall establish and maintain procedures to control

the design of the device in order to ensure that specified design requirements are met.

(2) The following class I devices are subject to design controls:

(i) Devices automated with computer software; and

(ii) The devices listed in the following chart.

Section	Device
868.6810	Catheter, Tracheobronchial Suction.
878.4460	Glove, Surgeon's.
880.6760	Restraint, Protective.
892.5650	System, Applicator, Radionuclide, Manual.
892.5740	Source, Radionuclide Teletherapy.

(b) *Design and development planning.* Each manufacturer shall establish and maintain plans that describe or reference the design and development activities and define responsibility for implementation. The plans shall identify and describe the interfaces with different groups or activities that provide, or result in, input to the design and development process. The plans shall be reviewed, updated, and approved as design and development evolves.

(c) *Design input.* Each manufacturer shall establish and maintain procedures to ensure that the design requirements relating to a device are appropriate and address the intended use of the device, including the needs of the user and patient. The procedures shall include a mechanism for addressing incomplete, ambiguous, or conflicting requirements. The design input requirements shall be documented and shall be reviewed and approved by a designated individual(s). The approval, including the date and signature of the individual(s) approving the requirements, shall be documented.

(d) *Design output.* Each manufacturer shall establish and maintain procedures for defining and documenting design output in terms that allow an adequate evaluation of conformance to design input requirements. Design output procedures shall contain or make reference to acceptance criteria and shall ensure that those design outputs that are essential for the proper functioning of the device are identified. Design output shall be documented, reviewed, and approved before release. The approval, including the date and signature of the individual(s) approving the output, shall be documented.

(e) *Design review.* Each manufacturer shall establish and maintain procedures to ensure that formal documented reviews of the design results are planned and conducted at appropriate stages of the device's design development. The procedures shall ensure that participants at each design review include representatives of all functions concerned with the design stage being reviewed and an individual(s) who does not have direct responsibility for the design stage being reviewed, as well as any specialists needed. The results of a design review, including identification of the design, the date, and the individual(s) performing the review, shall be documented in the design history file (the DHF).

(f) *Design verification.* Each manufacturer shall establish and maintain procedures for verifying the device design. Design verification shall confirm that the design output meets the design input requirements. The results of the design verification, including identification of the design, method(s), the date, and the individual(s) performing the verification, shall be documented in the DHF.

(g) *Design validation.* Each manufacturer shall establish and maintain procedures for validating the device design. Design validation shall be performed under defined operating conditions on initial production units, lots, or batches, or their equivalents. Design validation shall ensure that devices conform to defined user needs and intended uses and shall include testing of production units under actual or simulated use conditions. Design validation shall include software validation and risk analysis, where appropriate. The results of the design validation, including identification of the design, method(s), the date, and the individual(s) performing the validation, shall be documented in the DHF.

(h) *Design transfer.* Each manufacturer shall establish and maintain procedures to ensure that the device design is correctly translated into production specifications.

(i) *Design changes.* Each manufacturer shall establish and maintain procedures for the identification, documentation, validation or where appropriate verification, review, and approval of design changes before their implementation.

(j) *Design history file.* Each manufacturer shall establish and maintain a DHF for each type of device. The DHF shall contain or reference the records necessary to demonstrate that the design was developed in accordance with the approved design plan and the requirements of this part.

Subpart D--Document Controls

§820.40 Document controls.

Each manufacturer shall establish and maintain procedures to control all documents that are required by this part. The procedures shall provide for the following:

(a) *Document approval and distribution.* Each manufacturer shall designate an individual(s) to review for adequacy and approve prior to issuance all documents established to meet the requirements of this part. The approval, including the date and signature of the individual(s) approving the document, shall be documented. Documents established to meet the requirements of this part shall be available at all locations for which they are designated, used, or otherwise necessary, and all obsolete documents shall be promptly removed from all points of use or otherwise prevented from unintended use.

(b) *Document changes.* Changes to documents shall be reviewed and approved by an individual(s) in the same function or organization that performed the original review and approval, unless specifically designated otherwise. Approved changes shall be communicated to the appropriate personnel in a timely manner. Each manufacturer shall maintain records of changes to documents. Change records shall include a description of the change, identification of the affected documents, the signature of the approving individual(s), the approval date, and when the change becomes effective.

Subpart E--Purchasing Controls

§820.50 Purchasing controls.

Each manufacturer shall establish and maintain procedures to ensure that all purchased or otherwise received product and services conform to specified requirements.

(a) *Evaluation of suppliers, contractors, and consultants.* Each manufacturer shall establish and maintain the requirements, including quality requirements, that must be met by suppliers, contractors, and consultants. Each manufacturer shall:

(1) Evaluate and select potential suppliers, contractors, and consultants on the basis of their ability to meet specified requirements, including quality requirements. The evaluation shall be documented.

(2) Define the type and extent of control to be exercised over the product, services, suppliers, contractors, and consultants, based on the evaluation results.

(3) Establish and maintain records of acceptable suppliers, contractors, and consultants.

(b) *Purchasing data.* Each manufacturer shall establish and maintain data that clearly describe or reference the specified requirements, including quality requirements, for purchased or otherwise received product and services. Purchasing documents shall include, where possible, an agreement that the suppliers, contractors, and consultants agree to notify the manufacturer of changes in the product or service so that manufacturers may determine whether the changes may affect the quality of a finished device. Purchasing data shall be approved in accordance with §820.40.

Subpart F--Identification and Traceability

§820.60 Identification.

Each manufacturer shall establish and maintain procedures for identifying product during all stages of receipt, production, distribution, and installation to prevent mixups.

§820.65 Traceability.

Each manufacturer of a device that is intended for surgical implant into the body or to support or sustain life and whose failure to perform when properly used in accordance with instructions for use provided in the labeling can be reasonably expected to result in a significant injury to the user shall establish and maintain procedures for identifying with a control number each unit, lot, or batch of finished devices and where appropriate components. The procedures shall facilitate corrective action. Such identification shall be documented in the DHR.

Subpart G--Production and Process Controls

§820.70 Production and process controls.

(a) *General.* Each manufacturer shall develop, conduct, control, and monitor production processes to ensure that a device conforms to its specifications. Where deviations from device specifications could occur as a result of the manufacturing process, the manufacturer shall establish and maintain process control procedures that describe any process controls necessary to ensure conformance to specifications. Where process controls are needed they shall include:

(1) Documented instructions, standard operating procedures (SOP's), and methods that define and control the mannor of production;

(2) Monitoring and control of process parameters and component and device characteristics during production;

(3) Compliance with specified reference standards or codes;

(4) The approval of processes and process equipment; and

(5) Criteria for workmanship which shall be expressed in documented standards or by means of identified and approved representative samples.

(b) *Production and process changes.* Each manufacturer shall establish and maintain procedures for changes to a specification, method, process, or procedure. Such changes shall be verified or where appropriate validated according to §820.75, before implementation and these activities shall be documented. Changes shall be approved in accordance with §820.40.

(c) *Environmental control.* Where environmental conditions could reasonably be expected to have an adverse effect on product quality, the manufacturer shall establish and maintain procedures to adequately control these environmental conditions. Environmental control system(s) shall be periodically inspected to verify that the system, including necessary equipment, is adequate and functioning properly. These activities shall be documented and reviewed.

(d) *Personnel.* Each manufacturer shall establish and maintain requirements for the health, cleanliness, personal practices, and clothing of personnel if contact between such personnel and product or environment could reasonably be expected to have an adverse effect on product quality. The manufacturer shall ensure that maintenance and other personnel who are required to work temporarily under special environmental conditions are appropriately trained or supervised by a trained individual.

(e) *Contamination control.* Each manufacturer shall establish and maintain procedures to prevent contamination of equipment or product by substances that could reasonably be expected to have an adverse effect on product quality.

(f) *Buildings.* Buildings shall be of suitable design and contain sufficient space to perform necessary operations, prevent mixups, and assure orderly handling.

(g) *Equipment.* Each manufacturer shall ensure that all equipment used in the manufacturing process meets specified requirements and is appropriately designed, constructed, placed, and installed to facilitate maintenance, adjustment, cleaning, and use.

(1) *Maintenance schedule.* Each manufacturer shall establish and maintain schedules for the adjustment, cleaning, and other maintenance of equipment to ensure that manufacturing specifications are met. Maintenance activities, including the date and individual(s) performing the maintenance activities, shall be documented.

(2) *Inspection.* Each manufacturer shall conduct periodic inspections in accordance with established procedures to ensure adherence to applicable equipment maintenance schedules. The inspections, including the date and individual(s) conducting the inspections, shall be documented.

(3) *Adjustment.* Each manufacturer shall ensure that any inherent limitations or allowable tolerances are visibly posted on or near equipment requiring periodic adjustments or are readily available to personnel performing these adjustments.

(h) *Manufacturing material.* Where a manufacturing material could reasonably be expected to have an adverse effect on product quality, the manufacturer shall establish and maintain procedures for the use and removal of such manufacturing material to ensure that it is removed or limited to an amount that does not adversely affect the device's quality. The removal or reduction of such manufacturing material shall be documented.

(i) *Automated processes.* When computers or automated data processing systems are used as part of production or the quality system, the manufacturer shall validate computer software for its intended use according to an established protocol. All software changes shall be validated before approval and issuance. These validation activities and results shall be documented.

§820.72 Inspection, measuring, and test equipment.

(a) *Control of inspection, measuring, and test equipment.* Each manufacturer shall ensure that all inspection, measuring, and test equipment, including mechanical, automated, or electronic inspection and test equipment, is suitable for its intended purposes and is capable of producing valid results. Each manufacturer shall establish and maintain procedures to ensure that equipment is routinely calibrated, inspected, checked, and maintained. The procedures shall include provisions for handling, preservation, and storage of equipment, so that its accuracy and fitness for use are maintained. These activities shall be documented.

(b) *Calibration.* Calibration procedures shall include specific directions and limits for accuracy and precision. When accuracy and precision limits are not met, there shall be provisions for remedial action to reestablish the limits and to evaluate whether there was any adverse effect on the device's quality. These activities shall be documented.

(1) *Calibration standards.* Calibration standards used for inspection, measuring, and test equipment shall be traceable to national or international standards. If national or international standards are not practical or available, the manufacturer shall use an independent reproducible standard. If no applicable standard exists, the manufacturer shall establish and maintain an in-house standard.

(2) *Calibration records.* The equipment identification, calibration dates, the individual performing each calibration, and the next calibration date shall be documented. These records shall be displayed on or near each piece of equipment or shall be readily available to the personnel using such equipment and to the individuals responsible for calibrating the equipment.

§820.75 Process validation.

(a) Where the results of a process cannot be fully verified by subsequent inspection and test, the process shall be validated with a high degree of assurance and approved according to established procedures. The validation activities and results, including the date and signature of the individual(s) approving the validation and where appropriate the major equipment validated, shall be documented.

(b) Each manufacturer shall establish and maintain procedures for monitoring and control of process parameters for validated processes to ensure that the specified requirements continue to be met.

(1) Each manufacturer shall ensure that validated processes are performed by qualified individual(s).

(2) For validated processes, the monitoring and control methods and data, the date performed, and, where appropriate, the individual(s) performing the process or the major equipment used shall be documented.

(c) When changes or process deviations occur, the manufacturer shall review and evaluate the process and perform revalidation where appropriate. These activities shall be documented.

Subpart H--Acceptance Activities

§820.80 Receiving, in-process, and finished device acceptance.

(a) *General.* Each manufacturer shall establish and maintain procedures for acceptance activities. Acceptance activities include inspections, tests, or other verification activities.

(b) *Receiving acceptance activities.* Each manufacturer shall establish and maintain procedures for acceptance of incoming product. Incoming product shall be inspected, tested, or otherwise verified as conforming to specified requirements. Acceptance or rejection shall be documented.

(c) *In-process acceptance activities.* Each manufacturer shall establish and maintain acceptance procedures, where appropriate, to ensure that specified requirements for in-process product are met. Such procedures shall ensure that in-process product is controlled until the required inspection and tests or other verification activities have been completed, or necessary approvals are received, and are documented.

(d) *Final acceptance activities.* Each manufacturer shall establish and maintain procedures for finished device acceptance to ensure that each production run, lot, or batch of finished devices meets acceptance criteria. Finished devices shall be held in quarantine or otherwise adequately controlled until released. Finished devices shall not be released for distribution until:

(1) The activities required in the DMR are completed;

(2) the associated data and documentation is reviewed;

(3) the release is authorized by the signature of a designated individual(s); and

(4) the authorization is dated.

(e) *Acceptance records.* Each manufacturer shall document acceptance activities required by this part. These records shall include:

(1) The acceptance activities performed;

(2) the dates acceptance activities are performed;

(3) the results;

(4) the signature of the individual(s) conducting the acceptance activities; and

(5) where appropriate the equipment used. These records shall be part of the DHR.

§820.86   Acceptance status.

Each manufacturer shall identify by suitable means the acceptance status of product, to indicate the conformance or nonconformance of product with acceptance criteria. The identification of acceptance status shall be maintained throughout manufacturing, packaging, labeling, installation, and servicing of the product to ensure that only product which has passed the required acceptance activities is distributed, used, or installed.

Subpart I--Nonconforming Product

§820.90 Nonconforming product.

(a) *Control of nonconforming product.* Each manufacturer shall establish and maintain procedures to control product that does not conform to specified requirements. The procedures shall address the identification, documentation, evaluation, segregation, and disposition of nonconforming product. The evaluation of nonconformance shall include a determination of the need for an investigation and notification of the persons or organizations responsible for the nonconformance. The evaluation and any investigation shall be documented.

(b) *Nonconformity review and disposition.*

(1) Each manufacturer shall establish and maintain procedures that define the responsibility for review and the authority for the disposition of nonconforming product. The procedures shall set forth the review and disposition process. Disposition of nonconforming product shall be documented. Documentation shall include the justification for use of nonconforming product and the signature of the individual(s) authorizing the use.

(2) Each manufacturer shall establish and maintain procedures for rework, to include retesting and reevaluation of the nonconforming product after rework, to ensure that the product meets its current approved specifications. Rework and reevaluation activities, including a determination of any adverse effect from the rework upon the product, shall be documented in the DHR.

Subpart J--Corrective and Preventive Action

§820.100 Corrective and preventive action.

(a) Each manufacturer shall establish and maintain procedures for implementing corrective and preventive action. The procedures shall include requirements for:

(1) Analyzing processes, work operations, concessions, quality audit reports, quality records, service records, complaints, returned product, and other sources of quality

data to identify existing and potential causes of nonconforming product, or other quality problems. Appropriate statistical methodology shall be employed where necessary to detect recurring quality problems;

(2) Investigating the cause of nonconformities relating to product, processes, and the quality system;

(3) Identifying the action(s) needed to correct and prevent recurrence of nonconforming product and other quality problems;

(4) Verifying or validating the corrective and preventive action to ensure that such action is effective and does not adversely affect the finished device;

(5) Implementing and recording changes in methods and procedures needed to correct and prevent identified quality problems;

(6) Ensuring that information related to quality problems or nonconforming product is disseminated to those directly responsible for assuring the quality of such product or the prevention of such problems; and

(7) Submitting relevant information on identified quality problems, as well as corrective and preventive actions, for management review.

(b) All activities required under this section, and their results, shall be documented.

Subpart K--Labeling and Packaging Control

§820.120 Device labeling.

Each manufacturer shall establish and maintain procedures to control labeling activities.

(a) *Label integrity.* Labels shall be printed and applied so as to remain legible and affixed during the customary conditions of processing, storage, handling, distribution, and where appropriate use.

(b) *Labeling inspection.* Labeling shall not be released for storage or use until a designated individual(s) has examined the labeling for accuracy including, where applicable, the correct unique device identifier (UDI) or universal product code (UPC), expiration date, control number, storage instructions, handling instructions, and any additional processing instructions. The release, including the date and signature of the individual(s) performing the examination, shall be documented in the DHR.

(c) *Labeling storage.* Each manufacturer shall store labeling in a manner that provides proper identification and is designed to prevent mixups.

(d) *Labeling operations.* Each manufacturer shall control labeling and packaging operations to prevent labeling mixups. The label and labeling used for each production unit, lot, or batch shall be documented in the DHR.

(e) *Control number.* Where a control number is required by §820.65, that control number shall be on or shall accompany the device through distribution.

[61 FR 52654, Oct. 7, 1996, as amended at 78 FR 55822, Sept. 24, 2013]

§820.130 Device packaging.

Each manufacturer shall ensure that device packaging and shipping containers are designed and constructed to protect the device from alteration or damage during the customary conditions of processing, storage, handling, and distribution.

Subpart L--Handling, Storage, Distribution, and Installation

§820.140 Handling.

Each manufacturer shall establish and maintain procedures to ensure that mixups, damage, deterioration, contamination, or other adverse effects to product do not occur during handling.

§820.150 Storage.

(a) Each manufacturer shall establish and maintain procedures for the control of storage areas and stock rooms for product to prevent mixups, damage, deterioration, contamination, or other adverse effects pending use or distribution and to ensure that no obsolete, rejected, or deteriorated product is used or distributed. When the quality of product deteriorates over time, it shall be stored in a manner to facilitate proper stock rotation, and its condition shall be assessed as appropriate.

(b) Each manufacturer shall establish and maintain procedures that describe the methods for authorizing receipt from and dispatch to storage areas and stock rooms.

§820.160 Distribution.

(a) Each manufacturer shall establish and maintain procedures for control and distribution of finished devices to ensure that only those devices approved for release are distributed and that purchase orders are reviewed to ensure that ambiguities and errors are resolved before devices are released for distribution. Where a device's fitness for use or quality deteriorates over time, the procedures shall ensure that expired devices or devices deteriorated beyond acceptable fitness for use are not distributed.

(b) Each manufacturer shall maintain distribution records which include or refer to the location of:
 (1) The name and address of the initial consignee;
 (2) The identification and quantity of devices shipped;
 (3) The date shipped; and
 (4) Any control number(s) used.

§820.170 Installation.

(a) Each manufacturer of a device requiring installation shall establish and maintain adequate installation and inspection instructions, and where appropriate test procedures. Instructions and procedures shall include directions for ensuring proper installation so that the device will perform as intended after installation. The manufacturer shall distribute the instructions and procedures with the device or otherwise make them available to the person(s) installing the device.

(b) The person installing the device shall ensure that the installation, inspection, and any required testing are performed in accordance with the manufacturer's instructions and procedures and shall document the inspection and any test results to demonstrate proper installation.

Subpart M--Records

§820.180 General requirements.

All records required by this part shall be maintained at the manufacturing establishment or other location that is reasonably accessible to responsible officials of the manufacturer and to employees of FDA designated to perform inspections. Such records, including those not stored at the inspected establishment, shall be made readily available for review and copying by FDA employee(s). Such records shall be legible and shall be stored to minimize deterioration and to prevent loss. Those records stored in automated data processing systems shall be backed up.

(a) *Confidentiality.* Records deemed confidential by the manufacturer may be marked to aid FDA in determining whether information may be disclosed under the public information regulation in part 20 of this chapter.

(b) *Record retention period.* All records required by this part shall be retained for a period of time equivalent to the design and expected life of the device, but in no case less than 2 years from the date of release for commercial distribution by the manufacturer.

(c) *Exceptions.* This section does not apply to the reports required by §820.20(c) Management review, §820.22 Quality audits, and supplier audit reports used to meet the requirements of §820.50(a) Evaluation of suppliers, contractors, and consultants, but does apply to procedures established under these provisions. Upon request of a designated employee of FDA, an employee in management with executive responsibility shall certify in writing that the management reviews and quality audits required under this part, and supplier audits where applicable, have been performed and documented, the dates on which they were performed, and that any required corrective action has been undertaken.

§820.181 Device master record.

Each manufacturer shall maintain device master records (DMR's). Each manufacturer shall ensure that each DMR is prepared and approved in accordance with §820.40. The DMR for each type of device shall include, or refer to the location of, the following information:

(a) Device specifications including appropriate drawings, composition, formulation, component specifications, and software specifications;

(b) Production process specifications including the appropriate equipment specifications, production methods, production procedures, and production environment specifications;

(c) Quality assurance procedures and specifications including acceptance criteria and the quality assurance equipment to be used;

(d) Packaging and labeling specifications, including methods and processes used; and

(e) Installation, maintenance, and servicing procedures and methods.

§820.184 Device history record.

Each manufacturer shall maintain device history records (DHR's). Each manufacturer shall establish and maintain procedures to ensure that DHR's for each batch, lot, or unit are maintained to demonstrate that the device is manufactured in accordance with the DMR and the requirements of this part. The DHR shall include, or refer to the location of, the following information:

(a) The dates of manufacture;

(b) The quantity manufactured;

(c) The quantity released for distribution;

(d) The acceptance records which demonstrate the device is manufactured in accordance with the DMR;

(e) The primary identification label and labeling used for each production unit; and

(f) Any unique device identifier (UDI) or universal product code (UPC), and any other device identification(s) and control number(s) used.

[61 FR 52654, Oct. 7, 1996, as amended at 78 FR 55822, Sept. 24, 2013]

§820.186 Quality system record.

Each manufacturer shall maintain a quality system record (QSR). The QSR shall include, or refer to the location of, procedures and the documentation of activities required by this part that are not specific to a particular type of device(s), including, but not limited to, the records required by §820.20. Each manufacturer shall ensure that the QSR is prepared and approved in accordance with §820.40.

§820.198 Complaint files.

(a) Each manufacturer shall maintain complaint files. Each manufacturer shall establish and maintain procedures for receiving, reviewing, and evaluating complaints by a formally designated unit. Such procedures shall ensure that:

(1) All complaints are processed in a uniform and timely manner;

(2) Oral complaints are documented upon receipt; and

(3) Complaints are evaluated to determine whether the complaint represents an event which is required to be reported to FDA under part 803 of this chapter, Medical Device Reporting.

(b) Each manufacturer shall review and evaluate all complaints to determine whether an investigation is necessary. When no investigation is made, the manufacturer shall maintain a record that includes the reason no investigation was made and the name of the individual responsible for the decision not to investigate.

(c) Any complaint involving the possible failure of a device, labeling, or packaging to meet any of its specifications shall be reviewed, evaluated, and investigated, unless such investigation has already been performed for a similar complaint and another investigation is not necessary.

(d) Any complaint that represents an event which must be reported to FDA under part 803 of this chapter shall be promptly reviewed, evaluated, and investigated by a designated individual(s) and shall be maintained in a separate portion of the complaint files or otherwise clearly identified. In addition to the information required by §820.198(e), records of investigation under this paragraph shall include a determination of:

(1) Whether the device failed to meet specifications;

(2) Whether the device was being used for treatment or diagnosis; and

(3) The relationship, if any, of the device to the reported incident or adverse event.

(e) When an investigation is made under this section, a record of the investigation shall be maintained by the formally designated unit identified in paragraph (a) of this section. The record of investigation shall include:

(1) The name of the device;

(2) The date the complaint was received;

(3) Any unique device identifier (UDI) or universal product code (UPC), and any other device identification(s) and control number(s) used;

(4) The name, address, and phone number of the complainant;

(5) The nature and details of the complaint;

(6) The dates and results of the investigation;

(7) Any corrective action taken; and

(8) Any reply to the complainant.

(f) When the manufacturer's formally designated complaint unit is located at a site separate from the manufacturing establishment, the investigated complaint(s) and the record(s) of investigation shall be reasonably accessible to the manufacturing establishment.

(g) If a manufacturer's formally designated complaint unit is located outside of the United States, records required by this section shall be reasonably accessible in the United States at either:

(1) A location in the United States where the manufacturer's records are regularly kept; or

(2) The location of the initial distributor.

[61 FR 52654, Oct. 7, 1996, as amended at 69 FR 11313, Mar. 10, 2004; 71 FR 16228, Mar. 31, 2006; 78 FR 55822, Sept. 24, 2013]

Subpart N--Servicing

§820.200 Servicing.

(a) Where servicing is a specified requirement, each manufacturer shall establish and maintain instructions and procedures for performing and verifying that the servicing meets the specified requirements.

(b) Each manufacturer shall analyze service reports with appropriate statistical methodology in accordance with §820.100.

(c) Each manufacturer who receives a service report that represents an event which must be reported to FDA under part 803 of this chapter shall automatically consider the report a complaint and shall process it in accordance with the requirements of §820.198.

(d) Service reports shall be documented and shall include:

(1) The name of the device serviced;

(2) Any unique device identifier (UDI) or universal product code (UPC), and any other device identification(s) and control number(s) used;

(3) The date of service;

(4) The individual(s) servicing the device;

(5) The service performed; and

(6) The test and inspection data.

[61 FR 52654, Oct. 7, 1996, as amended at 69 FR 11313, Mar. 10, 2004; 78 FR 55822, Sept. 24, 2013]

Subpart O--Statistical Techniques

§820.250 Statistical techniques.

(a) Where appropriate, each manufacturer shall establish and maintain procedures for identifying valid statistical techniques required for establishing, controlling, and verifying the acceptability of process capability and product characteristics.

(b) Sampling plans, when used, shall be written and based on a valid statistical rationale. Each manufacturer shall establish and maintain procedures to ensure that sampling methods are adequate for their intended use and to ensure that when changes occur the sampling plans are reviewed. These activities shall be documented.

Notes

EU GMPs

EU Guidelines to GMP

INTRODUCTION
CHAPTER 1 • **PHARMACEUTICAL QUALITY SYSTEM**
CHAPTER 2 • **PERSONNEL**
CHAPTER 3 • **PREMISES AND EQUIPMENT**
CHAPTER 4 • **DOCUMENTATION**
CHAPTER 5 • **PRODUCTION**
CHAPTER 6 • **QUALITY CONTROL**
CHAPTER 7 • **CONTRACT MANUFACTURE AND ANALYSIS**
CHAPTER 8 • **COMPLAINTS AND PRODUCT RECALLS**
CHAPTER 9 • **SELF INSPECTION**
GLOSSARY

Printed by GMP Publications, Inc.
Tel: 866-544-9007 or 856-810-7331
Fax: 866-544-9002
http://www.gmppublications.com
sales@gmppublications.com

EudraLex

The Rules Governing Medicinal Products in the European Union

EU Guidelines to Good Manufacturing Practice Medicinal Products for Human and Veterinary Use

Introduction

Document History	
The first edition of the Guide was published, including an annex on the manufacture of sterile medicinal products.	1989
The second edition was published; implementing Commission Directives 91/356 of 13 June 1991 and 91/412 of 23 July 1991 laying down the principles and guidelines on good manufacturing practice for medicinal products for human use as well as for veterinary medicinal products. The second edition also included 12 additional annexes.	January 1992
An update of legal references was made. In the meantime, the guide is updated as needed on the website of the European Commission, several additional annexes added.	August 2004
Re-structuring of GMP guide, consisting of Part I for medicinal products for human and veterinary use and Part II for active substances used as starting materials, implementing Directives 2004/27/EC and 2004/28/EC. The current guide includes 17 Annexes, the former Annex 18 being replaced.	October 2005
Update of the text and introduction of a new Part III	December 2010

Introduction

The pharmaceutical industry of the European Union maintains high standards of Quality Management in the development, manufacture and control of medicinal products. A system of marketing authorisations ensures that all medicinal products are assessed by a competent authority to ensure compliance with contemporary requirements of safety, quality and efficacy. A system of manufacturing authorisations ensures that all products authorised on the European market are manufactured/ imported only by authorised manufacturers, whose activities are regularly inspected by the competent authorities, using Quality Risk Management principles. Manufacturing authorisations are required by all pharmaceutical manufacturers in the European Union whether the products are sold within or outside of the Union.

Two directives laying down principles and guidelines of good manufacturing practice (GMP) for medicinal products were adopted by the Commission. Directive 2003/94/EC applies to medicinal products for human use and Directive 91/412/EEC for veterinary use. Detailed guidelines in accordance with those principles are published in the Guide to Good Manufacturing Practice which will be used in assessing applications for manufacturing authorisations and as a basis for inspection of manufacturers of medicinal products.

The principles of GMP and the detailed guidelines are applicable to all operations which require the authorisations referred to in Article 40 of Directive 2001/83/EC, in Article 44 of Directive 2001/82/EC and Article 13 of Directive 2001/20/EC, as amended. They are also relevant for pharmaceutical manufacturing processes, such as that undertaken in hospitals.

All Member States and the industry agreed that the GMP requirements applicable to the manufacture of veterinary medicinal products are the same as those applicable to the manufacture of medicinal products for human use. Certain detailed adjustments to the GMP guidelines are set out in two annexes specific to veterinary medicinal products and to immunological veterinary medicinal products.

The Guide is presented in three parts and supplemented by a series of annexes. Part I covers GMP principles for the manufacture of medicinal products. Part II covers GMP for active substances used as starting materials. Part III contains GMP related documents, which clarify regulatory expectations.

Chapters of Part I on "basic requirements" are headed by principles as defined in Directives 2003/94/EC and 91/412/EEC. Chapter 1 on Quality Management outlines the fundamental concept of quality management as applied to the manufacture of medicinal products. Thereafter, each chapter has a principle outlining the quality management objectives of that chapter and a text which provides sufficient detail for manufacturers to be made aware of the essential matters to be considered when implementing the principle.

According to the revised Article 47 and Article 51, respectively, of the Directive 2001/83/EC and Directive 2001/82/EC, as amended, detailed guidelines on the principles of GMP for active substances used as starting materials shall be adopted and published by the Commission. Part II was established on the basis of a guideline developed on the level of ICH and published as ICH Q7A on "active pharmaceutical ingredients". It has an extended application both for the human and the veterinary sector.

In addition to the general matters of Good Manufacturing Practice outlined in Part I and II, a series of annexes providing detail about specific areas of activity is included. For some manufacturing processes, different annexes will apply simultaneously (e.g. annex on sterile preparations and on radiopharmaceuticals and/or on biological medicinal products).

A glossary of some terms used in the Guide has been incorporated after the annexes. Part III is intended to host a collection of GMP related documents, which are not detailed guidelines on the principles of GMP laid down in Directives 2003/94/EC and 91/412/EC. The aim of Part III is to clarify regulatory expectations and it should be viewed as a source of information on current best practices. Details on the applicability will be described separately in each document.

The Guide is not intended to cover safety aspects for the personnel engaged in manufacture. This may be particularly important in the manufacture of certain medicinal products such as highly active, biological and radioactive medicinal products. However, those aspects are governed by other provisions of Union or national law.

Throughout the Guide, it is assumed that the requirements of the Marketing Authorisation relating to the safety, quality and efficacy of the products, are systematically incorporated into all the manufacturing, control and release for sale arrangements of the holder of the Manufacturing Authorisation.

For many years, the manufacture of medicinal products has taken place in accordance with guidelines for Good Manufacturing Practice and the manufacture of medicinal products is not governed by CEN/ISO standards. The CEN/ISO standards have been considered but the terminology of these standards has not been implemented in this edition. It is recognised that there are acceptable methods, other than those described in the Guide, which are capable of achieving the principles of Quality Management. The Guide is not intended to place any restraint upon the development of any new concepts or new technologies which have been validated and which provide a level of Quality Management at least equivalent to those set out in this Guide.

The GMP guide will be regularly revised in order to reflect continual improvement of best practices in the field of Quality. Revisions will be made publicly available on the website of the European Commission: http://ec.europa.eu/health/documents/eudralex/vol-4/index_en.htm

EudraLex

The Rules Governing Medicinal Products in the European Union

Volume 4

EU Guidelines for Good Manufacturing Practice for Medicinal Products for Human and Veterinary Use

Chapter 1

Pharmaceutical Quality System

Legal basis for publishing the detailed guidelines:

Article 47 of Directive 2001/83/EC on the Community code relating to medicinal products for human use and Article 51 of Directive 2001/82/EC on the Community code relating to veterinary medicinal products. This document provides guidance for the interpretation of the principles and guidelines of good manufacturing practice (GMP) for medicinal products as laid down in Directive 2003/94/EC for medicinal products for human use and Directive 91/412/EEC for veterinary use.

Status of the document: revision 3

Reasons for changes: Amendments to the text of Chapter 1 have been made in order to align with the concepts and terminology described in the ICH Q10 tripartite guideline on Pharmaceutical Quality System. The title of the chapter itself is also changed accordingly.

Deadline for coming into operation: 31 January 2013

Principle

The holder of a Manufacturing Authorisation must manufacture medicinal products so as to ensure that they are fit for their intended use, comply with the requirements of the Marketing Authorisation or Clinical Trial Authorisation, as appropriate and do not place patients at risk due to inadequate safety, quality or efficacy. The attainment of this quality objective is the responsibility of senior management and requires the participation and commitment by staff in many different departments and at all levels within the company, by the company's suppliers and by its distributors. To achieve this quality objective reliably there must be a comprehensively designed and correctly implemented Pharmaceutical Quality System1 incorporating Good Manufacturing Practice and Quality Risk Management. It should be fully documented and its effectiveness monitored. All parts of the Pharmaceutical Quality System should be adequately resourced with competent personnel, and suitable and sufficient premises, equipment and facilities. There are additional legal responsibilities for the holder of the Manufacturing Authorisation and for the Qualified Person(s).

The basic concepts of Quality Management, Good Manufacturing Practice and Quality Risk Management are inter-related. They are described here in order to emphasise their relationships and their fundamental importance to the production and control of medicinal products.

Pharmaceutical Quality System[1]

1.1 Quality Management is a wide-ranging concept, which covers all matters, which individually or collectively influence the quality of a product. It is the sum total of the organised arrangements made with the objective of ensuring that medicinal products are of the quality required for their intended use. Quality Management therefore incorporates Good Manufacturing Practice.

1.2 GMP applies to the lifecycle stages from the manufacture of investigational medicinal products, technology transfer, commercial manufacturing through to product discontinuation. However the Pharmaceutical Quality System can extend to the pharmaceutical development lifecycle stage as described in ICH Q10, which while optional, should facilitate innovation and continual improvement and strengthen the link between pharmaceutical development and manufacturing activities. ICH Q10 is reproduced in Part III of the Guide and can be used to supplement the contents of this chapter.

1.3 The size and complexity of the company's activities should be taken into consideration when developing a new Pharmaceutical Quality System or modifying an existing one. The design of the system should incorporate appropriate risk management principles including the use of appropriate tools. While some aspects of the system can be company-wide and others site-specific, the effectiveness of the system is normally demonstrated at the site level.

---

[1] Art 6 of Directives 2003/94/EC and 91/412/EEC require manufacturers to establish and implement an effective pharmaceutical quality assurance system. The term Pharmaceutical Quality System is used in this chapter in the interests of consistency with ICH Q10 terminology. For the purposes of this chapter these terms can be considered interchangeable.

1.4 A Pharmaceutical Quality System appropriate for the manufacture of medicinal products should ensure that:

(i) Product realisation is achieved by designing, planning, implementing, maintaining and continuously improving a system that allows the consistent delivery of products with appropriate quality attributes;

(ii) Product and process knowledge is managed throughout all lifecycle stages;

(iii) Medicinal products are designed and developed in a way that takes account of the requirements of Good Manufacturing Practice;

(iv) Production and control operations are clearly specified and Good Manufacturing Practice adopted;

(v) Managerial responsibilities are clearly specified;

(vi) Arrangements are made for the manufacture, supply and use of the correct starting and packaging materials, the selection and monitoring of suppliers and for verifying that each delivery is from the approved supply chain;

(vii) Processes are in place to assure the management of outsourced activities.

(viii) A state of control is established and maintained by developing and using effective monitoring and control systems for process performance and product quality.

(ix) The results of product and processes monitoring are taken into account in batch release, in the investigation of deviations, and, with a view to taking preventive action to avoid potential deviations occurring in the future.

(x) All necessary controls on intermediate

products, and any other in-process controls and validations are carried out;

(xii) Continual improvement is facilitated through the implementation of quality improvements appropriate to the current level of process and product knowledge.

(xiii) Arrangements are in place for the prospective evaluation of planned changes and their approval prior to implementation taking into account regulatory notification and approval where required;

(xiv) After implementation of any change, an evaluation is undertaken to confirm the quality objectives were achieved and that there was no unintended deleterious impact on product quality;

(xv) An appropriate level of root cause analysis should be applied during the investigation of deviations, suspected product defects and other problems. This can be determined using Quality Risk Management principles. In cases where the true root cause(s) of the issue cannot be determined, consideration should be given to identifying the most likely root cause(s) and to addressing those. Where human error is suspected or identified as the cause, this should be justified having taken care to ensure that process, procedural or systembased errors or problems have not been overlooked, if present. Appropriate corrective actions and/or preventative actions (CAPAs) should be identified and taken in response to investigations. The effectiveness of such actions should be monitored and assessed, in line with Quality Risk Management principles.

(xv) Medicinal products are not sold or supplied before a Qualified Person has certified that each production batch has been produced and controlled in accordance with the requirements of the Marketing Authorisation and any other regulations relevant to the production, control and release of medicinal products;

(xvi) Satisfactory arrangements exist to ensure, as far as possible, that the medicinal products are stored, distributed and subsequently handled so that quality is maintained throughout their shelf life;

(xvii) There is a process for self-inspection and/or quality audit, which regularly appraises the effectiveness and applicability of the Pharmaceutical Quality System.

1.5 Senior management has the ultimate responsibility to ensure an effective Pharmaceutical Quality System is in place, adequately resourced and that roles, responsibilities, and authorities are defined, communicated and implemented throughout the organisation. Senior management's leadership and active participation in the Pharmaceutical Quality System is essential. This leadership should ensure the support and commitment of staff at all levels and sites within the organisation to the Pharmaceutical Quality System.

1.6 There should be periodic management review, with the involvement of senior management, of the operation of the Pharmaceutical Quality System to identify opportunities for continual improvement of products, processes and the system itself.

1.7 The Pharmaceutical Quality System should be defined and documented. A Quality Manual or equivalent documentation should be established and should contain a description of the quality management system including management responsibilities.

Good Manufacturing Practice for Medicinal Products

1.8 Good Manufacturing Practice is that part of Quality Management which ensures that products are consistently produced and controlled to the quality standards appropriate to their intended use and as required by the Marketing Authorisation, Clinical Trial Authorisation or product specification. Good Manufacturing Practice is concerned with both production and quality control. The basic requirements of GMP are that:

(i) All manufacturing processes are clearly defined, systematically reviewed in the light of experience and shown to be capable of consistently manufacturing medicinal products of the required quality and complying with their specifications;

(ii) Critical steps of manufacturing processes and significant changes to the process are validated;

(iii) All necessary facilities for GMP are provided including:

- Appropriately qualified and trained personnel;
- Adequate premises and space;
- Suitable equipment and services;
- Correct materials, containers and labels;
- Approved procedures and instructions, in accordance with the Pharmaceutical Quality System;
- Suitable storage and transport;

(iv) Instructions and procedures are written in an instructional form in clear and unambiguous language, specifically applicable to the facilities provided;

(v) Procedures are carried out correctly and operators are trained to do so;

(vi) Records are made, manually and/or by recording instruments, during manufacture which demonstrate that all the steps required by the defined procedures and instructions were in fact taken and that the quantity and quality of the product was as expected.

(vii) Any significant deviations are fully recorded, investigated with the objective of determining the root cause and appropriate corrective and preventive action implemented;

(viii) Records of manufacture including distribution which enable the complete history of a batch to be traced are retained in a comprehensible and accessible form;

(ix) The distribution of the products minimises any risk to their quality and takes account of Good Distribution Practice;

(x) A system is available to recall any batch of product, from sale or supply;

(xi) Complaints about products are examined, the causes of quality defects investigated and appropriate measures taken in respect of the defective products and to prevent reoccurrence.

Quality Control

1.9 Quality Control is that part of Good Manufacturing Practice which is concerned with sampling, specifications and testing, and with the organisation, documentation and release procedures which ensure that the necessary and relevant tests are actually carried out and that materials are not released for use, nor products released for sale or supply, until their quality has been judged to be satisfactory. The basic requirements of Quality Control are that:

(i) Adequate facilities, trained personnel and approved procedures are available for sampling and testing starting materials, packaging materials,

intermediate, bulk, and finished products, and where appropriate for monitoring environmental conditions for GMP purposes;

(ii) Samples of starting materials, packaging materials, intermediate products, bulk products and finished products are taken by approved personnel and methods;

(iii) Test methods are validated;

(iv) Records are made, manually and/or by recording instruments, which demonstrate that all the required sampling, inspecting and testing procedures

were actually carried out. Any deviations are fully recorded and investigated;

(v) The finished products contain active ingredients complying with the qualitative and quantitative composition of the Marketing Authorisation or clinical trial authorisation, are of the purity required, and are enclosed within their proper containers and correctly labelled;

(vi) Records are made of the results of inspection and that testing of materials, intermediate, bulk, and finished products is formally assessed against specification. Product assessment includes a review and evaluation of relevant production documentation and an assessment of deviations from specified procedures;

(vii) No batch of product is released for sale or supply prior to certification by a Qualified Person that it is in accordance with the requirements of the relevant authorisations in accordance with annex 16;

(viii) Sufficient reference samples of starting materials and products are retained in accordance with Annex 19 to permit future examination of the product if necessary and that the sample is retained in the final pack.

Product Quality Review

1.10 Regular periodic or rolling quality reviews of all authorised medicinal products, including export only products, should be conducted with the objective of verifying the consistency of the existing process, the appropriateness of current specifications for both starting materials and finished product, to highlight any trends and to identify product and process improvements. Such reviews should normally be conducted and documented annually, taking into account previous reviews, and should include at least:

(i) A review of starting materials including packaging materials used in the product, especially those from new sources and in particular the review of supply chain traceability of active substances.

(ii) A review of critical in-process controls and finished product results.

(iii) A review of all batches that failed to meet established specification(s) and their investigation.

(iv) A review of all significant deviations or non-conformances, their related investigations, and the effectiveness of resultant corrective and preventive actions taken.

(v) A review of all changes carried out to the processes or analytical methods.

(vi) A review of Marketing Authorisation variations submitted, granted or refused, including those for third country (export only) dossiers.

(vii) A review of the results of the stability monitoring programme and any adverse trends.

(viii) A review of all quality-related returns, complaints and recalls and the investigations performed at the time.

(ix) A review of adequacy of any other previous product process or equipment corrective actions.

(x) For new marketing authorisations and variations to marketing authorisations, a review of post-marketing commitments.

(xi) The qualification status of relevant equipment and utilities, e.g. HVAC, water, compressed gases, etc.

(xii) A review of any contractual arrangements as defined in Chapter 7 to ensure that they are up to date.

1.11 The manufacturer and, where different, marketing authorisation holder should evaluate the results of the review and an assessment made as to whether corrective and preventive action or any revalidation should be undertaken, under the Pharmaceutical Quality System. There should be management procedures for the ongoing management and review of these actions and the effectiveness of these procedures verified during self-inspection. Quality reviews may be grouped by product type, e.g. solid dosage forms, liquid dosage forms, sterile products, etc. where scientifically justified.

Where the marketing authorisation holder is not the manufacturer, there should be a technical agreement in place between the various parties that defines their respective responsibilities in producing the product quality review.

Quality Risk Management

1.12 Quality risk management is a systematic process for the assessment, control, communication and review of risks to the quality of the medicinal product. It can be applied both proactively and retrospectively.

1.13 The principles of quality risk management are that:

i) The evaluation of the risk to quality is based on scientific knowledge, experience with the process and ultimately links to the protection of the patient

ii) The level of effort, formality and documentation of the quality risk management process is commensurate with the level of risk Examples of the processes and applications of quality risk management can be found inter alia in ICH Q9 which is reproduced in Part III of the Guide.

Notes

EudraLex

The Rules Governing Medicinal Products in the European Union

Volume 4

EU Guidelines for Good Manufacturing Practice for Medicinal Products for Human and Veterinary Use

Part 1

<u>Chapter 2: Personnel</u>

Legal basis for publishing the detailed guidelines: Article 47 of Directive 2001/83/EC on the Community code relating to medicinal products for human use and Article 51 of Directive 2001/82/EC on the Community code relating to veterinary medicinal products. This document provides guidance for the interpretation of the principles and guidelines of good manufacturing practice (GMP) for medicinal products as laid down in Directive 2003/94/EC for medicinal products for human use and Directive 91/412/EEC for veterinary use.

Status of the document: Revision [a]

Reasons for changes: Changes have been made in order to integrate the principles of "Pharmaceutical Quality System" as described in the ICH Q10 tripartite guideline. A section has been added on consultants

Deadline for coming into operation: 16 February 2014

---

[a] On 26 March 2014 minor change to references to in paragraph 2.5 to other paragraphs of Chapter 2.

Principle

The correct manufacture of medicinal products relies upon people. For this reason there must be sufficient qualified personnel to carry out all the tasks which are the responsibility of the manufacturer. Individual responsibilities should be clearly understood by the individuals and recorded. All personnel should be aware of the principles of Good Manufacturing Practice that affect them and receive initial and continuing training, including hygiene instructions, relevant to their needs.

General

2.1 The manufacturer should have an adequate number of personnel with the necessary qualifications and practical experience. Senior management should determine and provide adequate and appropriate resources (human, financial, materials, facilities and equipment) to implement and maintain the quality management system and continually improve its effectiveness. The responsibilities placed on any one individual should not be so extensive as to present any risk to quality.

2.2 The manufacturer must have an organisation chart in which the relationships between the heads of Production, Quality Control and where applicable Head of Quality Assurance or Quality Unit referred to in point 2.5 and the position of the Qualified Person(s) are clearly shown in the managerial hierarchy.

2.3 People in responsible positions should have specific duties recorded in written job descriptions and adequate authority to carry out their responsibilities. Their duties may be delegated to designated deputies of a satisfactory qualification level. There should be no gaps or unexplained overlaps in the responsibilities of those personnel concerned with the application of Good Manufacturing Practice.

2.4 Senior management has the ultimate responsibility to ensure an effective quality management system is in place to achieve the quality objectives, and, that roles, responsibilities, and authorities are defined, communicated and implemented throughout the organisation. Senior management should establish a quality policy that describes the overall intentions and direction of the company related to quality and should ensure continuing suitability and effectiveness of the quality management system and GMP compliance through participation in management review.

Key Personnel

2.5 Senior Management should appoint Key Management Personnel including the head of Production, the head of Quality Control, and if at least one of these persons is not responsible for the duties described in Article 51 of Directive 2001/83/EC1, an adequate number, but at least one, Qualified Person(s) designated for the purpose. Normally, key posts should be occupied by full-time personnel. The heads of Production and Quality Control must be independent from each other. In large organisations, it may be necessary to delegate some of the functions listed in 2.7, 2.8 and 2.9. Additionally depending on the size and organisational structure of the company, a separate Head of Quality Assurance or Head of the Quality Unit may be appointed. Where such a function exists usually some of the responsibilities described in 2.7, 2.8 and 2.9 are shared with the Head of Quality Control and Head of Production and senior management should therefore take care that roles, responsibilities, and authorities are defined.

---

[1] Article 55 of Directive 2001/82/EC

2.6 The duties of the Qualified Person(s) are described in Article 51 of Directive 2001/83/EC, and can be summarised as follows:

a) for medicinal products manufactured within the European Union, a Qualified Person must ensure that each batch has been manufactured and checked in compliance with the laws in force in that Member State and in accordance with the requirements of the marketing authorisation [2];

(b) in the case of medicinal products coming from third countries, irrespective of whether the product has been manufactured in the European Union a Qualified Person must ensure that each production batch has undergone in a Member State a full qualitative analysis, a quantitative analysis of at least all the active substances and all the other tests or checks necessary to ensure the quality of medicinal products in accordance with the requirements of the marketing authorisation. The Qualified Person must certify in a register or equivalent document, as operations are carried out and before any release, that each production batch satisfies the provisions of Article 51.

The persons responsible for these duties must meet the qualification requirements laid down

in Article 49[3] of the same Directive, they shall be permanently and continuously at the disposal of the holder of the Manufacturing Authorisation to carry out their responsibilities.

The responsibilities of a Qualified Person may be delegated, but only to other Qualified Person(s).

Guidance on the role of the Qualified Person is elaborated in Annex 16.

---

[2] According to Article 51 paragraph 1 of Directive 2001/83/EC), the batches of medicinal products which have undergone such controls in a Member State shall be exempt from the controls if they are marketed in another Member State, accompanied by the control reports signed by the qualified person.

[3] Article 53 of Directive 2001/82/EC

2.7 The head of the Production Department generally has the following responsibilities:

i. To ensure that products are produced and stored according to the appropriate documentation in order to obtain the required quality;
ii. To approve the instructions relating to production operations and to ensure their strict implementation;
iii. To ensure that the production records are evaluated and signed by an authorised person;
iv. To ensure the qualification and maintenance of his department, premises and equipment;
v. To ensure that the appropriate validations are done;
vi. To ensure that the required initial and continuing training of his department personnel is carried out and adapted according to need.

2.8 The head of Quality Control generally has the following responsibilities:

i. To approve or reject, as he sees fit, starting materials, packaging materials, intermediate, bulk and finished products;
ii. To ensure that all necessary testing is carried out and the associated records evaluated;
iii. To approve specifications, sampling instructions, test methods and other Quality Control procedures;
iv. To approve and monitor any contract analysts;
v. To ensure the qualification and maintenance of his department, premises and equipment;
vi. To ensure that the appropriate validations are done;
vii. To ensure that the required initial and continuing training of his department personnel is carried out and adapted according to need.

Other duties of Quality Control are summarised in Chapter 6.

2.9 The heads of Production, Quality Control and where relevant, Head of Quality Assurance or Head of Quality Unit, generally have some shared, or jointly exercised, responsibilities relating to quality including in particular the design, effective implementation, monitoring and maintenance of the quality management system. These may include, subject to any national regulations:

i. The authorisation of written procedures and other documents, including amendments;
ii. The monitoring and control of the manufacturing environment;
iii. Plant hygiene;
iv. Process validation;
v. Training;
vi. The approval and monitoring of suppliers of materials;
vii. The approval and monitoring of contract manufacturers and providers of other GMP related outsourced activities;
viii. The designation and monitoring of storage conditions for materials and products;
ix. The retention of records;
x. The monitoring of compliance with the requirements of Good Manufacturing Practice;
xi. The inspection, investigation, and taking of samples, in order to monitor factors which may affect product quality;
xii. Participation in management reviews of process performance, product quality and of the quality management system and advocating continual improvement
xiii. Ensuring that a timely and effective communication and escalation process exists to raise quality issues to the appropriate levels of management.

Training

2.10 The manufacturer should provide training for all the personnel whose duties take them into production and storage areas or into control laboratories (including the technical, maintenance and cleaning personnel), and for other personnel whose activities could affect the quality of the product.

2.11 Besides the basic training on the theory and practice of the quality management system and Good Manufacturing Practice, newly recruited personnel should receive training appropriate to the duties assigned to them. Continuing training should also be given, and its practical effectiveness should be periodically assessed. Training programmes should be available, approved by either the head of Production or the head of Quality Control, as appropriate. Training records should be kept.

2.12 Personnel working in areas where contamination is a hazard, e.g. clean areas or areas where highly active, toxic, infectious or sensitising materials are handled, should be given specific training.

2.13 Visitors or untrained personnel should, preferably, not be taken into the production and quality control areas. If this is unavoidable, they should be given information in advance, particularly about personal hygiene and the prescribed protective clothing. They should be closely supervised.

2.14 The pharmaceutical quality system and all the measures capable of improving its understanding and implementation should be fully discussed during the training sessions.

Personnel Hygiene

2.15 Detailed hygiene programmes should be established and adapted to the different needs within the factory. They should include procedures relating to the health, hygiene practices and clothing of personnel. These procedures should be understood and followed in a very strict way by every person whose duties take him into the production and control areas. Hygiene programmes should be promoted by management and widely discussed during training sessions.

2.16 All personnel should receive medical examination upon recruitment. It must be the manufacturer's responsibility that there are instructions ensuring that health conditions that can be of relevance to the quality of products come to the manufacturer's knowledge. After the first medical examination, examinations should be carried out when necessary for the work and personal health.

2.17 Steps should be taken to ensure as far as is practicable that no person affected by an infectious disease or having open lesions on the exposed surface of the body is engaged in the manufacture of medicinal products.

2.18 Every person entering the manufacturing areas should wear protective garments appropriate to the operations to be carried out.

2.19 Eating, drinking, chewing or smoking, or the storage of food, drink, smoking materials or personal medication in the production and storage areas should be prohibited. In general, any unhygienic practice within the manufacturing areas or in any other area where the product might be adversely affected should be forbidden.

2.20 Direct contact should be avoided between the operator's hands and the exposed product as well as with any part of the equipment that comes into contact with the products.

2.21 Personnel should be instructed to use the hand-washing facilities.

2.22 Any specific requirements for the manufacture of special groups of products, for example sterile preparations, are covered in the annexes. Consultants

2.23 Consultants should have adequate education, training, and experience, or any combination thereof, to advise on the subject for which they are retained.

Records should be maintained stating the name, address, qualifications, and type of service provided by these consultants.

EudraLex

The Rules Governing Medicinal Products in the European Union

Volume 4

EU Guidelines for Good Manufacturing Practice for Medicinal Products for Human and Veterinary Use

Part 1

Chapter 3: Premises and Equipment

Legal basis for publishing the detailed guidelines: Article 47 of Directive 2001/83/EC on the Community code relating to medicinal products for human use and Article 51 of Directive 2001/82/EC on the Community code relating to veterinary medicinal products. This document provides guidance for the interpretation of the principles and guidelines of good manufacturing practice (GMP) for medicinal products as laid down in Directive 2003/94/EC for medicinal products for human use and Directive 91/412/EEC for veterinary use.

Status of the document: Revision [a].

Reasons for changes: The only change is to section 6 as part of the improved guidance on prevention of cross-contamination involving also Chapter 5.

Deadline for coming into operation: 1 March 2015. However, the toxicological evaluation mentioned in section 6 is to be carried out:

---

[a] In January 2015 the deadline for coming into operation was adapted with regard to the toxicological evaluation to align with the coming effect of the EMA guideline on setting health based exposure limits for use in risk identification in the manufacture of different medicinal products in shared facilities.

- from 1 June 2015 onwards for any medicinal product newly introduced into shared manufacturing facilities;

- before 1 December 2015 for medicinal products already produced in a shared manufacturing facility producing only medicinal products for human use or both producing medicinal products for human use and veterinary medicinal products on 31 May 2015;

- before 1 June 2016 for veterinary medicinal products already produced in a shared manufacturing facility producing only veterinary medicinal products on 31 May 2015.

PRINCIPLE

Premises and equipment must be located, designed, constructed, adapted and maintained to suit the operations to be carried out. Their layout and design must aim to minimise the risk of errors and permit effective cleaning and maintenance in order to avoid cross-contamination, build-up of dust or dirt and, in general, any adverse effect on the quality of products.

PREMISES

General

3.1 Premises should be situated in an environment which, when considered together with measures to protect the manufacture, presents minimal risk of causing contamination of materials or products.

3.2 Premises should be carefully maintained, ensuring that repair and maintenance operations do not present any hazard to the quality of products. They should be cleaned and, where applicable, disinfected according to detailed written procedures.

3.3 Lighting, temperature, humidity and ventilation should be appropriate and such that they do not adversely affect, directly or indirectly, either the medicinal products during their manufacture and storage, or the accurate functioning of equipment.

3.4 Premises should be designed and equipped so as to afford maximum protection against the entry of insects or other animals.

3.5 Steps should be taken in order to prevent the entry of unauthorised people. Production, storage and quality control areas should not be used as a right of way by personnel who do not work in them.

Production Area

3.6 Cross-contamination should be prevented for all products by appropriate design and operation of manufacturing facilities. The measures to prevent cross-contamination should be commensurate with the risks. Quality Risk Management principles should be used to assess and control the risks.
Depending of the level of risk, it may be necessary to dedicate premises and equipment for manufacturing and/or packaging operations to control the risk presented by some medicinal products.

Dedicated facilities are required for manufacturing when a medicinal product presents a risk because:

i. the risk cannot be adequately controlled by operational and/ or technical measures,

ii. scientific data from the toxicological evaluation does not support a controllable risk (e.g. allergenic potential from highly sensitising materials such as beta lactams) or

iii. relevant residue limits, derived from the toxicological evaluation, cannot be satisfactorily determined by a validated analytical method.

Further guidance can be found in Chapter 5 and in Annexes 2, 3, 4, 5 & 6.

3.7 Premises should preferably be laid out in such a way as to allow the production to take place in areas connected in a logical order corresponding to the sequence of the operations and to the requisite cleanliness levels.

3.8 The adequacy of the working and in-process storage space should permit the orderly and logical positioning of equipment and materials so as to minimise the risk of confusion between different medicinal products or their components, to avoid cross-contamination and to minimise the risk of omission or wrong application of any of the manufacturing or control steps.

3.9 Where starting and primary packaging materials, intermediate or bulk products are exposed to the environment, interior surfaces (walls, floors and ceilings) should be smooth, free from cracks and open joints, and should not shed particulate matter and should permit easy and effective cleaning and, if necessary, disinfection.

3.10 Pipework, light fittings, ventilation points and other services should be designed and sited to avoid the creation of recesses which are difficult to clean. As far as possible, for maintenance purposes, they should be accessible from outside the manufacturing areas.

3.11 Drains should be of adequate size, and have trapped gullies. Open channels should be avoided where possible, but if necessary, they should be shallow to facilitate cleaning and disinfection.

3.12 Production areas should be effectively ventilated, with air control facilities (including temperature and, where necessary, humidity and filtration) appropriate both to the products handled, to the operations undertaken within them and to the external environment.

3.13 Weighing of starting materials usually should be carried out in a separate weighing room designed for such use.

3.14 In cases where dust is generated (e.g. during sampling, weighing, mixing and processing operations, packaging of dry products), specific provisions should be taken to avoid cross-contamination and facilitate cleaning.

3.15 Premises for the packaging of medicinal products should be specifically designed and laid out so as to avoid mix-ups or cross-contamination.

3.16 Production areas should be well lit, particularly where visual on-line controls are carried out.

3.17 In-process controls may be carried out within the production area provided they do not carry any risk to production.

Storage Areas

3.18 Storage areas should be of sufficient capacity to allow orderly storage of the various categories of materials and products: starting and packaging materials, intermediate, bulk and finished products, products in quarantine, released, rejected, returned or recalled.

3.19 Storage areas should be designed or adapted to ensure good storage conditions. In particular, they should be clean and dry and maintained within acceptable temperature limits. Where special storage conditions are required (e.g. temperature, humidity) these should be provided, checked and monitored.

3.20 Receiving and dispatch bays should protect materials and products from the weather. Reception areas should be designed and equipped to allow containers of incoming materials to be cleaned where necessary before storage.

3.21 Where quarantine status is ensured by storage in separate areas, these areas must be clearly marked and their access restricted to authorised personnel. Any system replacing the physical quarantine should give equivalent security.

3.22 There should normally be a separate sampling area for starting materials. If sampling is performed in the storage area, it should be conducted in such a way as to prevent contamination or cross-contamination.

3.23 Segregated areas should be provided for the storage of rejected, recalled or returned materials or products.

3.24 Highly active materials or products should be stored in safe and secure areas.

3.25 Printed packaging materials are considered critical to the conformity of the medicinal product and special attention should be paid to the safe and secure storage of these materials.

Quality Control Areas

3.26 Normally, Quality Control laboratories should be separated from production areas. This is particularly important for laboratories for the control of biologicals, microbiologicals and radioisotopes, which should also be separated from each other.

3.27 Control laboratories should be designed to suit the operations to be carried out in them. Sufficient space should be given to avoid mix-ups and cross-contamination. There should be adequate suitable storage space for samples and records.

3.28 Separate rooms may be necessary to protect sensitive instruments from vibration, electrical interference, humidity, etc.

3.29 Special requirements are needed in laboratories handling particular substances, such as biological or radioactive samples.

Ancillary Areas

3.30 Rest and refreshment rooms should be separate from other areas.

3.31 Facilities for changing clothes and for washing and toilet purposes should be easily accessible and appropriate for the number of users. Toilets should not directly communicate with production or storage areas.

3.32 Maintenance workshops should as far as possible be separated from production areas. Whenever parts and tools are stored in the production area, they should be kept in rooms or lockers reserved for that use.

3.33 Animal houses should be well isolated from other areas, with separate entrance (animal access) and air handling facilities.

EQUIPMENT

3.34 Manufacturing equipment should be designed, located and maintained to suit its intended purpose.

3.35 Repair and maintenance operations should not present any hazard to the quality of the products.

3.36 Manufacturing equipment should be designed so that it can be easily and thoroughly cleaned. It should be cleaned according to detailed and written procedures and stored only in a clean and dry condition.

3.37 Washing and cleaning equipment should be chosen and used in order not to be a source of contamination.

3.38 Equipment should be installed in such a way as to prevent any risk of error or of contamination.

3.39 Production equipment should not present any hazard to products. Parts of production equipment that come into contact with the product must not be reactive, additive or absorptive to such an extent that it will affect the quality of the product and thus present any hazard.

3.40 Balances and measuring equipment of an appropriate range and precision should be available for production and control operations.

3.41 Measuring, weighing, recording and control equipment should be calibrated and checked at defined intervals by appropriate methods. Adequate records of such tests should be maintained.

3.42 Fixed pipework should be clearly labelled to indicate the contents and, where applicable, the direction of flow.

3.43 Distilled, deionised and, where appropriate, other water pipes should be sanitised according to written procedures that detail the action limits for microbiological contamination and the measures to be taken.

3.44 Defective equipment should, if possible, be removed from production and quality control areas, or at least be clearly labelled as defective.

CHAPTER 4 DOCUMENTATION - 30 June 2011

Table of Contents
Principle
Required GMP Documentation
Generation and Control of Documentation
Good Documentation Practices
Retention of Documents
Specifications
Manufacturing Formula and Processing Instructions
Procedures and records

Principle
Good documentation constitutes an essential part of the quality assurance system and is key to operating in compliance with GMP requirements. The various types of documents and media used should be fully defined in the manufacturer's Quality Management System. Documentation may exist in a variety of forms, including paper-based, electronic or photographic media. The main objective of the system of documentation utilized must be to establish, control, monitor and record all activities which directly or indirectly impact on all aspects of the quality of medicinal products. The Quality Management System should include sufficient instructional detail to facilitate a common understanding of the requirements, in addition to providing for sufficient recording of the various processes and evaluation of any observations, so that ongoing application of the requirements may be demonstrated.

There are two primary types of documentation used to manage and record GMP compliance: instructions (directions, requirements) and records/reports. Appropriate good documentation practice should be applied with respect to the type of document.

Suitable controls should be implemented to ensure the accuracy, integrity, availability and legibility of documents. Instruction documents should be free from errors and available in writing. The term 'written' means recorded, or documented on media from which data may be rendered in a human readable form.

Required GMP documentation (by type):

Site Master File: A document describing the GMP related activities of the manufacturer.

Instructions (directions, or requirements) type:

Specifications Describe in detail the requirements with which the products or materials used or obtained during manufacture have to conform. They serve as a basis for quality evaluation.

Manufacturing Formulae, Processing, Packaging and Testing Instructions: Provide detail all the starting materials, equipment and computerised systems (if any) to be used and specify all processing, packaging, sampling and testing instructions. In-process controls and process analytical technologies to be employed should be specified where relevant, together with acceptance criteria.

Procedures: (Otherwise known as Standard Operating Procedures, or SOPs), give directions for performing certain operations.

Protocols: Give instructions for performing and recording certain discreet operations.

Technical Agreements: Are agreed between contract givers and acceptors for outsourced activities.

Record/Report type:

Records: Provide evidence of various actions taken to demonstrate compliance with instructions, e.g. activities, events, investigations, and in the case of manufactured batches a history of each batch of product, including its distribution. Records include the raw data which is used to generate other records. For electronic records regulated users should define which data are to be used as raw data. At least, all data on which quality decisions are based should be defined as raw data.

Certificates of Analysis: Provide a summary of testing results on samples of products or materials[1] together with the evaluation for compliance to a stated specification.

Reports: Document the conduct of particular exercises, projects or investigations, together with results, conclusions and recommendations.

Generation and Control of Documentation

4.1 All types of document should be defined and adhered to. The requirements apply equally to all forms of document media types. Complex systems need to be understood, well documented, validated, and adequate controls should be in place. Many documents (instructions and/or records) may exist in hybrid forms, i.e. some elements as electronic and others as paper based. Relationships and control measures for master documents, official copies, data handling and records need to be stated for both hybrid and homogenous systems. Appropriate controls for electronic documents such as templates, forms, and master documents should be implemented. Appropriate controls should be in place to ensure the integrity of the record throughout the retention period.

4.2 Documents should be designed, prepared, reviewed, and distributed with care. They should comply with the relevant parts of Product Specification Files, Manufacturing and Marketing Authorisation dossiers, as appropriate. The reproduction of working documents from master documents should not allow any error to be introduced through the reproduction process.

---

[1] Alternatively the certification may be based, in-whole or in-part, on the assessment of real time data (summaries and exception reports) from batch related process analytical technology (PAT), parameters or metrics as per the approved marketing authorisation dossier.

4.3 Documents containing instructions should be approved, signed and dated by appropriate and authorised persons. Documents should have unambiguous contents and be uniquely identifiable. The effective date should be defined.

4.4 Documents containing instructions should be laid out in an orderly fashion and be easy to check. The style and language of documents should fit with their intended use. Standard Operating Procedures, Work Instructions and Methods should be written in an imperative mandatory style.

4.5 Documents within the Quality Management System should be regularly reviewed and kept up-to-date.

4.6 Documents should not be hand-written; although, where documents require the entry of data, sufficient space should be provided for such entries.

Good Documentation Practices
4.7 Handwritten entries should be made in clear, legible, indelible way.

4.8 Records should be made or completed at the time each action is taken and in such a way that all significant activities concerning the manufacture of medicinal products are traceable.

4.9 Any alteration made to the entry on a document should be signed and dated; the alteration should permit the reading of the original information. Where appropriate, the reason for the alteration should be recorded.

Retention of Documents
4.10 It should be clearly defined which record is related to each manufacturing activity and where this record is located. Secure controls must be in place to ensure the integrity of the record throughout the retention period and validated where appropriate.

4.11 Specific requirements apply to batch documentation which must be kept for one year after expiry of the batch to which it relates or at least five years after certification of the batch by the Qualified Person, whichever is the longer. For investigational medicinal products, the batch documentation must be kept for at least five years after the completion or formal discontinuation of the last clinical trial in which the batch was used. Other requirements for retention of documentation may be described in legislation in relation to specific types of product (e.g. Advanced Therapy Medicinal Products) and specify that longer retention periods be applied to certain documents.

4.12 For other types of documentation, the retention period will depend on the business activity which the documentation supports. Critical documentation, including raw data (for example relating to validation or stability), which supports information in the Marketing Authorisation should be retained whilst the authorization remains in force. It may be considered acceptable to retire certain documentation (e.g. raw data supporting validation reports or stability reports) where the data has been superseded by a full set of new data. Justification for this should be documented and should take into account the requirements for retention of batch documentation; for example, in the case of process validation data, the accompanying raw data should be retained for a period at least as long as the records for all batches whose release has been supported on the basis of that validation exercise.

The following section gives some examples of required documents. The quality management system should describe all documents required to ensure product quality and patient safety.

Specifications
4.13 There should be appropriately authorised and dated specifications for starting and packaging materials, and finished products.

Specifications for starting and packaging materials

4.14 Specifications for starting and primary or printed packaging materials should include or provide reference to, if applicable:
  a) A description of the materials, including:
       - The designated name and the internal code reference;
       - The reference, if any, to a pharmacopoeial monograph;
       - The approved suppliers and, if reasonable, the original producer of the material;
       - A specimen of printed materials;
  b) Directions for sampling and testing;
  c) Qualitative and quantitative requirements with acceptance limits;
  d) Storage conditions and precautions;
  e) The maximum period of storage before re-examination.

Specifications for intermediate and bulk products

4.15 Specifications for intermediate and bulk products should be available for critical steps or if these are purchased or dispatched. The specifications should be similar to specifications for starting materials or for finished products, as appropriate.

Specifications for finished products

4.16 Specifications for finished products should include or provide reference to:
  a) The designated name of the product and the code reference where applicable;
  b) The formula;
  c) A description of the pharmaceutical form and package details;
  d) Directions for sampling and testing
  e) The qualitative and quantitative requirements, with the acceptance limits;
  f) The storage conditions and any special handling precautions, where applicable;
  g) The shelf-life.

Manufacturing Formula and Processing Instructions

Approved, written Manufacturing Formula and Processing Instructions should exist for each product and batch size to be manufactured.

4.17 The Manufacturing Formula should include:
  a) The name of the product, with a product reference code relating to its specification;
  b) A description of the pharmaceutical form, strength of the product and batch size;
  c) A list of all starting materials to be used, with the amount of each, described; mention should be made of any substance that may disappear in the course of processing;
  d) A statement of the expected final yield with the acceptable limits, and of relevant intermediate yields, where applicable

4.18 The Processing Instructions should include:
  a) A statement of the processing location and the principal equipment to be used;
  b) The methods, or reference to the methods, to be used for preparing the critical equipment (e.g. cleaning, assembling, calibrating, sterilising);
  c) Checks that the equipment and work station are clear of previous products, documents or materials not required for the planned process, and that equipment is clean and suitable for use;
  d) Detailed stepwise processing instructions [e.g. checks on materials, pre-treatments, sequence for adding materials, critical process parameters (time, temp etc)];
  e) The instructions for any in-process controls with their limits;
  f) Where necessary, the requirements for bulk storage of the products; including the container, labeling and special storage conditions where applicable;
  g) Any special precautions to be observed.

Packaging Instructions

4.19 Approved Packaging Instructions for each product, pack size and type should exist. These should include, or have a reference to, the following:
  a) Name of the product; including the batch number of bulk and finished product
  b) Description of its pharmaceutical form, and strength where applicable;
  c) The pack size expressed in terms of the number, weight or volume of the product in the final container;
  d) A complete list of all the packaging materials required, including quantities, sizes and types, with the code or reference number relating to the specifications of each packaging material;
  e) Where appropriate, an example or reproduction of the relevant printed packaging materials, and specimens indicating where to apply batch number references, and shelf life of the product;
  f) Checks that the equipment and work station are clear of previous products, documents or materials not required for the planned packaging operations (line clearance), and that equipment is clean and suitable for use.
  g) Special precautions to be observed, including a careful examination of the area and equipment in order to ascertain the line clearance before operations begin;
  h) A description of the packaging operation, including any significant subsidiary operations, and equipment to be used;
  i) Details of in-process controls with instructions for sampling and acceptance limits.

Batch Processing Record

4.20 A Batch Processing Record should be kept for each batch processed. It should be based on the relevant parts of the currently approved Manufacturing Formula and Processing Instructions, and should contain the following information:

a) The name and batch number of the product;
b) Dates and times of commencement, of significant intermediate stages and of completion of production;
c) Identification (initials) of the operator(s) who performed each significant step of the process and, where appropriate, the name of any person who checked these operations;
d) The batch number and/or analytical control number as well as the quantities of each starting material actually weighed (including the batch number and amount of any recovered or reprocessed material added);
e) Any relevant processing operation or event and major equipment used;
f) A record of the in-process controls and the initials of the person(s) carrying them out, and the results obtained;
g) The product yield obtained at different and pertinent stages of manufacture;
h) Notes on special problems including details, with signed authorisation for any deviation from the Manufacturing Formula and Processing Instructions;
i) Approval by the person responsible for the processing operations.

Note: Where a validated process is continuously monitored and controlled, then automatically generated reports may be limited to compliance summaries and exception/ out-of-specification (OOS) data reports.

Batch Packaging Record
4.21 A Batch Packaging Record should be kept for each batch or part batch processed. It should be based on the relevant parts of the Packaging Instructions.
The batch packaging record should contain the following information:
a) The name and batch number of the product,
b) The date(s) and times of the packaging operations;
c) Identification (initials) of the operator(s) who performed each significant step of the process and, where appropriate, the name of any person who checked these operations;

d) Records of checks for identity and conformity with the packaging instructions, including the results of in-process controls;
e) Details of the packaging operations carried out, including references to equipment and the packaging lines used;
f) Whenever possible, samples of printed packaging materials used, including specimens of the batch coding, expiry dating and any additional overprinting;
g) Notes on any special problems or unusual events including details, with signed authorisation for any deviation from the Packaging Instructions;
h) The quantities and reference number or identification of all printed packaging materials and bulk product issued, used, destroyed or returned to stock and the quantities of obtained product, in order to provide for an adequate reconciliation. Where there are there are robust electronic controls in place during packaging there may be justification for not including this information
i) Approval by the person responsible for the packaging operations

Procedures and records

Receipt
4.22 There should be written procedures and records for the receipt of each delivery of each starting material, (including bulk, intermediate or finished goods), primary, secondary and printed packaging materials.

4.23 The records of the receipts should include:
a) The name of the material on the delivery note and the containers;
b) The "in-house" name and/or code of material (if different from a);
c) Date of receipt;
d) Supplier's name and, manufacturer's name;
e) Manufacturer's batch or reference number;
f) Total quantity and number of containers received;

g) The batch number assigned after receipt;
h) Any relevant comment.

4.24 There should be written procedures for the internal labeling, quarantine and storage of starting materials, packaging materials and other materials, as appropriate.

Sampling
4.25 There should be written procedures for sampling, which include the methods and equipment to be used, the amounts to be taken and any precautions to be observed to avoid contamination of the material or any deterioration in its quality.

Testing
4.26 There should be written procedures for testing materials and products at different stages of manufacture, describing the methods and equipment to be used. The tests performed should be recorded.

Other
4.27 Written release and rejection procedures should be available for materials and products, and in particular for the certification for sale of the finished product by the Qualified Person(s). All records should be available to the Qualified Person. A system should be in place to indicate special observations and any changes to critical data.

4.28 Records should be maintained for the distribution of each batch of a product in order to facilitate recall of any batch, if necessary.

4.29 There should be written policies, procedures, protocols, reports and the associated records of actions taken or conclusions reached, where appropriate, for the following examples:

- Validation and qualification of processes, equipment and systems;
- Equipment assembly and calibration;

- Technology transfer;
- Maintenance, cleaning and sanitation;
- Personnel matters including signature lists, training in GMP and technical matters, clothing and hygiene and verification of the effectiveness of training.
- Environmental monitoring;
- Pest control;
- Complaints;
- Recalls;
- Returns;
- Change control;
- Investigations into deviations and non-conformances;
- Internal quality/GMP compliance audits;
- Summaries of records where appropriate (e.g. product quality review);
- Supplier audits.

4.30 Clear operating procedures should be available for major items of manufacturing and test equipment.

4.31 Logbooks should be kept for major or critical analytical testing, production equipment, and areas where product has been processed. They should be used to record in chronological order, as appropriate, any use of the area, equipment/method, calibrations, maintenance, cleaning or repair operations, including the dates and identity of people who carried these operations out.

4.32 An inventory of documents within the Quality Management System should be maintained.

EudraLex

The Rules Governing Medicinal Products in the European Union

Volume 4 EU Guidelines for Good Manufacturing Practice for Medicinal Products for Human and Veterinary Use

Part 1

Chapter 5: Production

Legal basis for publishing the detailed guidelines: Article 47 of Directive 2001/83/EC on the Community code relating to medicinal products for human use and Article 51 of Directive 2001/82/EC on the Community code relating to veterinary medicinal products. This document provides guidance for the interpretation of the principles and guidelines of good manufacturing practice (GMP) for medicinal products as laid down in Directive 2003/94/EC for medicinal products for human use and Directive 91/412/EEC for veterinary use.

Status of the document: Revision [a].

Reasons for changes: Changes have been made to sections 17 to 21, including adding a new section, to improve the guidance on prevention of cross-contamination and to refer to toxicological assessment. Changes were also introduced in sections 27 to 30, including adding a new section, on the qualification of suppliers in order to reflect the legal obligation of manufacturing authorisation holders to ensure that active substances are produced in accordance with GMP. The changes include supply chain traceability.

---

[a] In January 2015 the deadline for coming into operation was adapted with regard to the toxicological evaluation to align with the coming effect of the EMA guideline on setting health based exposure limits for use in risk identification in the manufacture of different medicinal products in shared facilities. Furthermore, correction of the reference in footnote 2 took place.

Sections 35 and 36 are inserted to clarify and harmonise expectations of manufacturers regarding the testing of starting materials while section 71 introduces guidance on notification of restrictions in supply.

Deadline for coming into operation: 1 March 2015. However, the toxicological evaluation mentioned in section 20 has to be carried out:

- from 1 June 2015 onwards for any medicinal product newly introduced into shared manufacturing facilities;

- before 1 December 2015 for medicinal products already produced in a shared manufacturing facility producing only medicinal products for human use or producing both medicinal products for human use and veterinary medicinal products on 31 May 2015;

- before 1 June 2016 for veterinary medicinal products already produced in a shared manufacturing facility producing only veterinary medicinal products on 31 May 2015.

Principle

Production operations must follow clearly defined procedures; they must comply with the principles of Good Manufacturing Practice in order to obtain products of the requisite quality and be in accordance with the relevant manufacturing and marketing authorisations.

General

5.1 Production should be performed and supervised by competent people.

5.2 All handling of materials and products, such as receipt and quarantine, sampling, storage, labelling, dispensing, processing, packaging and distribution should be done in accordance with written procedures or instructions and, where necessary, recorded.

5.3 All incoming materials should be checked to ensure that the consignment corresponds to the order. Containers should be cleaned where necessary and labelled with the prescribed data.

5.4 Damage to containers and any other problem which might adversely affect the quality of a material should be investigated, recorded and reported to the Quality Control Department.

5.5 Incoming materials and finished products should be physically or administratively quarantined immediately after receipt or processing, until they have been released for use or distribution.

5.6 Intermediate and bulk products purchased as such should be handled on receipt as though they were starting materials.

5.7 All materials and products should be stored under the appropriate conditions established by the manufacturer and in an orderly fashion to permit batch segregation and stock rotation.

5.8 Checks on yields, and reconciliation of quantities, should be carried out as necessary to ensure that there are no discrepancies outside acceptable limits.

5.9 Operations on different products should not be carried out simultaneously or consecutively in the same room unless there is no risk of mix-up or cross-contamination.

5.10 At every stage of processing, products and materials should be protected from microbial and other contamination.

5.11 When working with dry materials and products, special precautions should be taken to prevent the generation and dissemination of dust. This applies particularly to the handling of highly active or sensitising materials.

5.12 At all times during processing, all materials, bulk containers, major items of equipment and where appropriate rooms used should be labelled or otherwise identified with an indication of the product or material being processed, its strength (where applicable) and batch number. Where applicable, this indication should also mention the stage of production.

5.13 Labels applied to containers, equipment or premises should be clear, unambiguous and in the company's agreed format. It is often helpful in addition to the wording on the labels to use colours to indicate status (for example, quarantined, accepted, rejected, clean).

5.14 Checks should be carried out to ensure that pipelines and other pieces of equipment used for the transportation of products from one area to another are connected in a correct manner.

5.15 Any deviation from instructions or procedures should be avoided as far as possible. If a deviation occurs, it should be approved in writing by a competent person, with the involvement of the Quality Control department when appropriate.

5.16 Access to production premises should be restricted to authorised personnel.

Prevention of cross-contamination in production

5.17 Normally, the production of non-medicinal products should be avoided in areas and with equipment destined for the production of medicinal products but, where justified, could be allowed where the measures to prevent cross-contamination with medicinal products described below and in Chapter 3 can be applied. The production and/or storage of technical poisons, such as pesticides (except where these are used for manufacture of medicinal products) and herbicides, should not be allowed in areas used for the manufacture and / or storage of medicinal products.

5.18 Contamination of a starting material or of a product by another material or product should be prevented. This risk of accidental cross-contamination resulting from the uncontrolled release of dust, gases, vapours, aerosols, genetic material or organisms from active substances, other starting materials, and products in process, from residues on equipment, and from operators' clothing should be assessed. The significance of this risk varies with the nature of the contaminant and that of the product being contaminated. Products in which cross-contamination is likely to be most significant are those administered by injection and those given over a long time. However, contamination of all products poses a risk to patient safety dependent on the nature and extent of contamination.

5.19 Cross-contamination should be prevented by attention to design of the premises and equipment as described in Chapter 3. This should be supported by attention to process design and implementation of any relevant technical or organizational measures, including effective and reproducible cleaning processes to control risk of cross-contamination.

5.20 A Quality Risk Management process, which includes a potency and toxicological evaluation, should be used to assess and control the cross-contamination risks presented by the products manufactured. Factors including; facility/equipment design and use, personnel and material flow, microbiological controls, physico-chemical characteristics of the active substance, process characteristics, cleaning processes and analytical capabilities relative to the relevant limits established from the evaluation of the products should also be taken into account. The outcome of the Quality Risk Management process should be the basis for determining the necessity for and extent to which premises and equipment should be dedicated to a particular product or product family. This may include dedicating specific product contact parts or dedication of the entire manufacturing facility. It may be acceptable to confine manufacturing activities to a segregated, self contained production area within a multiproduct facility, where justified.

5.21 The outcome of the Quality Risk Management process should be the basis for determining the extent of technical and organisational measures required to control risks for cross-contamination. These could include, but are not limited to, the following:

Technical Measures

i. Dedicated manufacturing facility (premises and equipment);

ii. Self-contained production areas having separate processing equipment and separate heating, ventilation and air-conditioning (HVAC) systems. It may also be desirable to isolate certain utilities from those used in other areas;

iii. Design of manufacturing process, premises and equipment to minimize opportunities for cross-contamination during processing, maintenance and cleaning;

iv. Use of "closed systems" for processing and material/product transfer between equipment;

v. Use of physical barrier systems, including isolators, as containment measures;

vi. Controlled removal of dust close to source of the contaminant e.g. through localised extraction;

vii. Dedication of equipment, dedication of product contact parts or dedication of selected parts which are harder to clean (e.g. filters), dedication of maintenance tools;

viii. Use of single use disposable technologies;

ix. Use of equipment designed for ease of cleaning;

x. Appropriate use of air-locks and pressure cascade to confine potential airborne contaminant within a specified area;

xi. Minimising the risk of contamination caused by recirculation or re-entry of untreated or insufficiently treated air;

xii. Use of automatic clean in place systems of validated effectiveness;

xiii. For common general wash areas, separation of equipment washing, drying and storage areas.

Organisational Measures

i. Dedicating the whole manufacturing facility or a self contained production area on a campaign basis (dedicated by separation in time) followed by a cleaning process of validated effectiveness;

ii. Keeping specific protective clothing inside areas where products with high risk of cross-contamination are processed;

iii. Cleaning verification after each product campaign should be considered as a detectability tool to support effectiveness of the Quality Risk Management approach for products deemed to present higher risk;

iv. Depending on the contamination risk, verification of cleaning of non product contact surfaces and monitoring of air within the manufacturing area and/or adjoining areas in order to demonstrate effectiveness of control measures against airborne contamination or contamination by mechanical transfer;

v. Specific measures for waste handling, contaminated rinsing water and soiled gowning;

vi. Recording of spills, accidental events or deviations from procedures;

vii. Design of cleaning processes for premises and equipment such that the cleaning processes in themselves do not present a cross-contamination risk;

viii. Design of detailed records for cleaning processes to assure completion of cleaning in accordance with approved procedures and use of cleaning status labels on equipment and manufacturing areas;

ix. Use of common general wash areas on a campaign basis;

x. Supervision of working behaviour to ensure training effectiveness and compliance with the relevant procedural controls.

5.22 Measures to prevent cross-contamination and their effectiveness should be reviewed periodically according to set procedures.

Validation

5.23 Validation studies should reinforce Good Manufacturing Practice and be conducted in accordance with defined procedures. Results and conclusions should be recorded.

5.24 When any new manufacturing formula or method of preparation is adopted, steps should be taken to demonstrate its suitability for routine processing. The defined process, using the materials and equipment specified, should be shown to yield a product consistently of the required quality.

5.25 Significant amendments to the manufacturing process, including any change in equipment or materials, which may affect product quality and/or the reproducibility of the process, should be validated.

5.26 Processes and procedures should undergo periodic critical re-validation to ensure that they remain capable of achieving the intended results.

Starting materials

5.27 The selection, qualification, approval and maintenance of suppliers of starting materials, together with their purchase and acceptance, should be documented as part of the pharmaceutical quality system. The level of supervision should be proportionate to the risks posed by the individual materials, taking account of their source, manufacturing process, supply chain complexity and the final use to which the material is put in the medicinal product. The supporting evidence for each supplier / material approval should be maintained. Staff involved in these activities should have a current knowledge of the suppliers, the supply chain and the associated risks involved. Where possible, starting materials should be purchased directly from the manufacturer of the starting material.

5.28 The quality requirements established by the manufacturer for the starting materials should be discussed and agreed with the suppliers. Appropriate aspects of the production, testing and control, including handling, labelling, packaging and distribution requirements, complaints, recalls and rejection procedures should be documented in a formal quality agreement or specification.

5.29 For the approval and maintenance of suppliers of active substances and excipients, the following is required:

Active substances [1]

Supply chain traceability should be established and the associated risks, from active substance starting materials to the finished medicinal product, should be formally assessed

---

[1] Specific requirements apply to the importation of active substances to be used in the manufacture of medicinal products for human use in article 46b of Directive 2001/83/EC.

and periodically verified. Appropriate measures should be put in place to reduce risks to the quality of the active substance.

The supply chain and traceability records for each active substance (including active substance starting materials) should be available and be retained by the EEA based manufacturer or importer of the medicinal product.

Audits should be carried out at the manufacturers and distributors of active substances to confirm that they comply with the relevant good manufacturing practice and good distribution practice requirements. The holder of the manufacturing authorisation shall verify such compliance either by himself or through an entity acting on his behalf under a contract. For veterinary medicinal products, audits should be conducted based on risk.

Audits should be of an appropriate duration and scope to ensure that a full and clear assessment of GMP is made; consideration should be given to potential cross-contamination from other materials on site. The report should fully reflect what was done and seen on the audit with any deficiencies clearly identified. Any required corrective and preventive actions should be implemented.

Further audits should be undertaken at intervals defined by the quality risk management process to ensure the maintenance of standards and continued use of the approved supply chain.

Excipients

Excipients and excipient suppliers should be controlled appropriately based on the results of a formalised quality risk assessment in accordance with the European Commission 'Guidelines on the formalised risk assessment for ascertaining the appropriate Good Manufacturing Practice for excipients of medicinal products for human use'.

5.30 For each delivery of starting material the containers should be checked for integrity of package, including tamper evident seal where relevant, and for correspondence between the delivery note, the purchase order, the supplier's labels and approved manufacturer and supplier information maintained by the medicinal product manufacturer. The receiving checks on each delivery should be documented.

5.31 If one material delivery is made up of different batches, each batch must be considered as separate for sampling, testing and release.

5.32 Starting materials in the storage area should be appropriately labelled (see section 13). Labels should bear at least the following information:

i. The designated name of the product and the internal code reference where applicable;

ii. A batch number given at receipt;

iii. Where appropriate, the status of the contents (e.g. in quarantine, on test, released, rejected);

iv. Where appropriate, an expiry date or a date beyond which retesting is necessary.
When fully computerised storage systems are used, all the above information need not necessarily be in a legible form on the label.

5.33 There should be appropriate procedures or measures to assure the identity of the contents of each container of starting material. Bulk containers from which samples have been drawn should be identified (see Chapter 6).

5.34 Only starting materials which have been released by the Quality Control department and which are within their retest period should be used.

5.35 Manufacturers of finished products are responsible for any testing of starting materials [2] as described In the marketing authorisation dossier.

---

[2] A similar approach should apply to packaging materials as stated in section 5.45

They can utilise partial or full test results from the approved starting material manufacturer but must, as a minimum, perform identification testing [3] of each batch according to Annex 8.

5.36 The rationale for the outsourcing of this testing should be justified and documented and the following requirements should be fulfilled:

i. Special attention should be paid to the distribution controls (transport, wholesaling, storage and delivery) in order to maintain the quality characteristics of the starting materials and to ensure that test results remain applicable to the delivered material;

ii. The medicinal product manufacturer should perform audits, either itself or via third parties, at appropriate intervals based on risk at the site(s) carrying out the testing (including sampling) of the starting materials in order to assure compliance with Good Manufacturing Practice and with the specifications and testing methods described in the marketing authorisation dossier;

iii. The certificate of analysis provided by the starting material manufacturer/supplier should be signed by a designated person with appropriate qualifications and experience. The signature assures that each batch has been checked for compliance with the agreed product specification unless this assurance is provided separately;

iv. The medicinal product manufacturer should have appropriate experience in dealing with the starting material manufacturer (including experience via a supplier) including assessment of batches previously received and the history of compliance before reducing in-house testing. Any significant change in the manufacturing or testing processes should be considered;

---

[3] Identity testing of starting materials should be performed according to the methods and the specifications of the relevant marketing authorisation dossier.

v. The medicinal product manufacturer should also perform (or via a separately approved contract laboratory) a full analysis at appropriate intervals based on risk and compare the results with the material manufacturer or supplier's certificate of analysis in order to check the reliability of the latter. Should this testing identify any discrepancy then an investigation should be performed and appropriate measures taken. The acceptance of certificates of analysis from the material manufacturer or supplier should be discontinued until these measures are completed.

5.37 Starting materials should only be dispensed by designated persons, following a written procedure, to ensure that the correct materials are accurately weighed or measured into clean and properly labelled containers.

5.38 Each dispensed material and its weight or volume should be independently checked and the check recorded.

5.39 Materials dispensed for each batch should be kept together and conspicuously labelled as such.

Processing operations: intermediate and bulk products

5.40 Before any processing operation is started, steps should be taken to ensure that the work area and equipment are clean and free from any starting materials, products, product residues or documents not required for the current operation.

5.41 Intermediate and bulk products should be kept under appropriate conditions.

5.42 Critical processes should be validated (see "Validation" in this Chapter).

5.43 Any necessary in-process controls and environmental controls should be carried out and recorded.

5.44 Any significant deviation from the expected yield should be recorded and investigated.

Packaging materials

5.45 The selection, qualification, approval and maintenance of suppliers of primary and printed packaging materials shall be accorded attention similar to that given to starting materials.

5.46 Particular attention should be paid to printed materials. They should be stored in adequately secure conditions such as to exclude unauthorised access. Cut labels and other loose printed materials should be stored and transported in separate closed containers so as to avoid mix-ups. Packaging materials should be issued for use only by authorised personnel following an approved and documented procedure.

5.47 Each delivery or batch of printed or primary packaging material should be given a specific reference number or identification mark.

5.48 Outdated or obsolete primary packaging material or printed packaging material should be destroyed and this disposal recorded.

Packaging operations

5.49 When setting up a programme for the packaging operations, particular attention should be given to minimising the risk of cross-contamination, mix-ups or substitutions. Different products should not be packaged in close proximity unless there is physical segregation.

5.50 Before packaging operations are begun, steps should be taken to ensure that the work area, packaging lines, printing machines and other equipment are clean and free from any products, materials or documents previously used, if these are not required for the current operation. The line-clearance should be performed according to an appropriate check-list.

5.51 The name and batch number of the product being handled should be displayed at each packaging station or line.

5.52 All products and packaging materials to be used should be checked on delivery to the packaging department for quantity, identity and conformity with the Packaging Instructions.

5.53 Containers for filling should be clean before filling. Attention should be given to avoid and remove any contaminants such as glass fragments and metal particles.

5.54 Normally, filling and sealing should be followed as quickly as possible by labelling. If it is not the case, appropriate procedures should be applied to ensure that no mix-ups or mislabelling can occur.

5.55 The correct performance of any printing operation (for example code numbers, expiry dates) to be done separately or in the course of the packaging should be checked and recorded. Attention should be paid to printing by hand which should be re-checked at regular intervals.

5.56 Special care should be taken when using cut-labels and when over-printing is carried out off-line. Roll-feed labels are normally preferable to cut-labels, in helping to avoid mix-ups.

5.57 Checks should be made to ensure that any electronic code readers, label counters or similar devices are operating correctly.

5.58 Printed and embossed information on packaging materials should be distinct and resistant to fading or erasing.

5.59 On-line control of the product during packaging should include at least checking the following:

i. General appearance of the packages;

ii. Whether the packages are complete;

iii. Whether the correct products and packaging materials are used;

iv. Whether any over-printing is correct;

v. Correct functioning of line monitors.

Samples taken away from the packaging line should not be returned.

5.60 Products which have been involved in an unusual event should only be reintroduced into the process after special inspection, investigation and approval by authorised personnel. Detailed record should be kept of this operation.

5.61 Any significant or unusual discrepancy observed during reconciliation of the amount of bulk product and printed packaging materials and the number of units produced should be investigated and satisfactorily accounted for before release.

5.62 Upon completion of a packaging operation, any unused batch-coded packaging materials should be destroyed and the destruction recorded. A documented procedure should be followed if un-coded printed materials are returned to stock.

Finished products

5.63 Finished products should be held in quarantine until their final release under conditions established by the manufacturer.

5.64 The evaluation of finished products and documentation which is necessary before release of product for sale is described in Chapter 6 (Quality Control).

5.65 After release, finished products should be stored as usable stock under conditions established by the manufacturer.

Rejected, recovered and returned materials

5.66 Rejected materials and products should be clearly marked as such and stored separately in restricted areas. They should either be returned to the suppliers or, where appropriate, reprocessed or destroyed. Whatever action is taken should be approved and recorded by authorised personnel.

5.67 The reprocessing of rejected products should be exceptional. It is only permitted if the quality of the final product is not affected, if the specifications are met and if it is done in accordance with a defined and authorised procedure after evaluation of the risks involved. Record should be kept of the reprocessing.

5.68 The recovery of all or part of earlier batches which conform to the required quality by incorporation into a batch of the same product at a defined stage of manufacture should be authorised beforehand. This recovery should be carried out in accordance with a defined procedure after evaluation of the risks involved, including any possible effect on shelf life. The recovery should be recorded.

5.69 The need for additional testing of any finished product which has been reprocessed, or into which a recovered product has been incorporated, should be considered by the Quality Control Department.

5.70 Products returned from the market and which have left the control of the manufacturer should be destroyed unless without doubt their quality is satisfactory; they may be considered for re-sale, re-labelling or recovery in a subsequent batch only after they have been critically assessed by the Quality Control Department in accordance with a written procedure. The nature of the product, any special storage conditions it requires, its condition and history, and the time elapsed since it was issued should all be taken into account in this assessment. Where any doubt arises over the quality of the product, it should not be considered suitable for re-issue or re-use, although basic chemical reprocessing to recover active ingredient may be possible. Any action taken should be appropriately recorded.

Product shortage due to manufacturing constraints

5.71 The manufacturer should report to the marketing authorisation holder (MAH) any constraints in manufacturing operations which may result in abnormal restriction in the supply. This should be done in a timely manner to facilitate reporting of the restriction in supply by the MAH, to the relevant competent authorities, in accordance with its legal obligations [4].

---

[4] Articles 23a and 81 of Directive 2001/83/EC

EudraLex

The Rules Governing Medicinal Products in the European Union

Volume 4

EU Guidelines for Good Manufacturing Practice for Medicinal Products for Human and Veterinary Use

Part 1

Chapter 6: Quality Control

Legal basis for publishing the detailed guidelines: Article 47 of Directive 2001/83/EC on the Community code relating to medicinal products for human use and Article 51 of Directive 2001/82/EC on the Community code relating to veterinary medicinal products. This document provides guidance for the interpretation of the principles and guidelines of good manufacturing practice (GMP) for medicinal products as laid down in Directive 2003/94/EC for medicinal products for human use and Directive 91/412/EEC for veterinary use.

Status of the document: Revision

Reasons for changes:
Inclusion of a new section on technical transfer of testing methods and other items such as Out Of Specification results.

Deadline for coming into operation: 1 October 2014

Principle

This chapter should be read in conjunction with all relevant sections of the GMP guide

Quality Control is concerned with sampling, specifications and testing as well as the organisation, documentation and release procedures which ensure that the necessary and relevant tests are carried out, and that materials are not released for use, nor products released for sale or supply, until their quality has been judged satisfactory. Quality Control is not confined to laboratory operations, but must be involved in all decisions which may concern the quality of the product. The independence of Quality Control from Production is considered fundamental to the satisfactory operation of Quality Control.

General

6.1 Each holder of a manufacturing authorisation should have a Quality Control Department. This department should be independent from other departments, and under the authority of a person with appropriate qualifications and experience, who has one or several control laboratories at his disposal. Adequate resources must be available to ensure that all the Quality Control arrangements are effectively and reliably carried out.

6.2 The principal duties of the head of Quality Control are summarised in Chapter 2. The Quality Control Department as a whole will also have other duties, such as to establish, validate and implement all quality control procedures, oversee the control of the reference and/or retention samples of materials and products when applicable, ensure the correct labelling of containers of materials and products, ensure the monitoring of the stability of the products, participate in theinvestigation of complaints related to the quality of the product, etc. All these operations should be carried out in accordance with written procedures and, where necessary, recorded.

6.3 Finished product assessment should embrace all relevant factors, including production conditions, results of in-process testing, a review of manufacturing (including packaging) documentation, compliance with Finished Product Specification and examination of the final finished pack.

6.4 Quality Control personnel should have access to production areas for sampling and investigation as appropriate.

Good Quality Control Laboratory Practice

6.5 Control laboratory premises and equipment should meet the general and specific requirements for Quality Control areas given in Chapter 3. Laboratory equipment should not be routinely moved between high risk areas to avoid accidental cross-contamination. In particular, the microbiological laboratory should be arranged so as to minimize risk of cross-contamination.

6.6 The personnel, premises, and equipment in the laboratories should be appropriate to the tasks imposed by the nature and the scale of the manufacturing operations. The use of outside laboratories, in conformity with the principles detailed in Chapter 7, Contract Analysis, can be accepted for particular reasons, but this should be stated in the Quality Control records.

Documentation

6.7 Laboratory documentation should follow the principles given in Chapter 4. An important part of this documentation deals with Quality Control and the following details should be readily available to the Quality Control Department:

i. Specifications;

ii. Procedures describing sampling, testing, records (including test worksheets and/or laboratory notebooks), recording and verifying;

iii. Procedures for and records of the calibration/qualification of instruments and maintenance of equipment;

iv. A procedure for the investigation of Out of Specification and Out Of Trend results;

v. Testing reports and/or certificates of analysis;

vi. Data from environmental (air, water and other utilities) monitoring, where required;

vii. Validation records of test methods, where applicable.

6.8 Any Quality Control documentation relating to a batch record should be retained following the principles given in chapter 4 on retention of batch documentation.

6.9 Some kinds of data (e.g. tests results, yields, environmental controls) should be recorded in a manner permitting trend evaluation. Any out of trend or out of specification data should be addressed and subject to investigation.

6.10 In addition to the information which is part of the batch documentation, other raw data such as laboratory notebooks and/or records should be retained and readily available

Sampling

6.11 The sample taking should be done and recorded in accordance with approved written procedures
that describe:

i. The method of sampling;

ii. The equipment to be used;

iii. The amount of the sample to be taken;

iv. Instructions for any required sub-division of the sample;

v. The type and condition of the sample container to be used;

vi. The identification of containers sampled;

vii. Any special precautions to be observed, especially with regard to the sampling of sterile
or noxious materials;

viii. The storage conditions;

ix. Instructions for the cleaning and storage of sampling equipment.

6.12 Samples should be representative of the batch of materials or products from which they are taken. Other samples may also be taken to monitor the most stressed part of a process (e.g. beginning or end of a process). The sampling plan used should be appropriately justified and based on a risk management approach.

6.13 Sample containers should bear a label indicating the contents, with the batch number, the date of sampling and the containers from which samples have been drawn. They should be managed in a manner to minimize the risk of mix-up and to protect the samples from adverse storage conditions.

6.14 Further guidance on reference and retention samples is given in Annex 19.

Testing

6.15 Testing methods should be validated. A laboratory that is using a testing method and which did not perform the original validation, should verify the appropriateness of the testing method. All testing operations described in the marketing authorisation or technical dossier should be carried out according to the approved methods.

6.16 The results obtained should be recorded. Results of parameters identified as quality attribute or as critical should be trended and checked to make sure that they are consistent with each other.
Any calculations should be critically examined.

6.17 The tests performed should be recorded and the records should include at least the following data:

i. Name of the material or product and, where applicable, dosage form;

ii. Batch number and, where appropriate, the manufacturer and/or supplier;

iii. References to the relevant specifications and testing procedures;

iv. Test results, including observations and calculations, and reference to any certificates of analysis;

v. Dates of testing;

vi. Initials of the persons who performed the testing;

vii. Initials of the persons who verified the testing and the calculations, where appropriate;

viii. A clear statement of approval or rejection (or other status decision) and the dated signature of the designated responsible person;

ix. Reference to the equipment used.

6.18 All the in-process controls, including those made in the production area by production personnel, should be performed according to methods approved by Quality Control and the results recorded.

6.19 Special attention should be given to the quality of laboratory reagents, solutions, glassware, reference standards and culture media. They should be prepared and controlled in accordance with written procedures. The level of controls should be commensurate to their use and to the available stability data.

6.20 Reference standards should be established as suitable for their intended use. Their qualification and certification as such should be clearly stated and documented. Whenever compendial reference standards from an officially recognised source exist, these should preferably be used as primary reference standards unless fully justified (the use of secondary standards is permitted once their traceability to primary standards has been demonstrated and is documented). These compendial materials should be used for the purpose described in the appropiate monograph unless otherwise authorised by the National Competent Authority.

6.21 Laboratory reagents, solutions, reference standards and culture media should be marked with the preparation and opening date and the signature of the person who prepared them. The expiry date of reagents and culture media should be indicated on the label, together with specific storage conditions. In addition, for volumetric solutions, the last date of standardisation and the last current factor should be indicated.

6.22 Where necessary, the date of receipt of any substance used for testing operations (e.g. reagents, solutions and reference standards) should be indicated on the container. Instructions for use and storage should be followed. In certain cases it may be necessary to carry out an identification test and/or other testing of reagent materials upon receipt or before use.

6.23 Culture media should be prepared in accordance with the media manufacturer's requirements unless scientifically justified. The performance of all culture media should be verified prior to use.

6.24 Used microbiological media and strains should be decontaminated according to a standard procedure and disposed of in a manner to prevent the cross-contamination and retention of residues. The in-use shelf life of microbiological media should be established, documented and scientifically justified.

6.25 Animals used for testing components, materials or products, should, where appropriate, be quarantined before use. They should be maintained and controlled in a manner that assures their suitability for the intended use. They should be identified, and adequate records should be maintained, showing the history of their use.

On-going stability programme

6.26 After marketing, the stability of the medicinal product should be monitored according to a continuous appropriate programme that will permit the detection of any stability issue (e.g. changes in levels of impurities or dissolution profile) associated with the formulation in the marketed package.

6.27 The purpose of the on-going stability programme is to monitor the product over its shelf life and to determine that the product remains, and can be expected to remain, within specifications under the labelled storage conditions.

6.28 This mainly applies to the medicinal product in the package in which it is sold, but consideration should also be given to the inclusion in the programme of bulk product. For example, when the bulk product is stored for a long period before being packaged and/or shipped from a manufacturing site to a packaging site, the impact on the stability of the packaged product should be evaluated and studied under ambient conditions. In addition, consideration should be given to intermediates that are stored and used over prolonged periods. Stability studies on reconstituted product are performed during product development and need not be monitored on an on-going basis. However, when relevant, the stability of reconstituted product can also be monitored.

6.29 The on-going stability programme should be described in a written protocol following the general rules of Chapter 4 and results formalised as a report. The equipment used for the ongoing stability programme (stability chambers among others) should be qualified and maintained following the general rules of Chapter 3 and Annex 15.

6.30 The protocol for an on-going stability programme should extend to the end of the shelf life period and should include, but not be limited to, the following parameters:

i. Number of batch(es) per strength and different batch sizes, if applicable;

ii. Relevant physical, chemical, microbiological and biological test methods;

iii. Acceptance criteria;

iv. Reference to test methods;

v. Description of the container closure system(s);

vi. Testing intervals (time points);

vii. Description of the conditions of storage (standardised ICH/VICH conditions for long term testing, consistent with the product labelling, should be used);

viii. Other applicable parameters specific to the medicinal product.

6.31 The protocol for the on-going stability programme can be different from that of the initial longterm stability study as submitted in the marketing authorisation dossier provided that this is justified and documented in the protocol (for example the frequency of testing, or when updating to ICH/VICH recommendations).

6.32 The number of batches and frequency of testing should provide a sufficient amount of data to allow for trend analysis. Unless otherwise justified, at least one batch per year of product manufactured in every strength and every primary packaging type, if relevant, should be included in the stability programme (unless none are produced during that year). For products where on-going stability monitoring would normally require testing using animals and no appropriate alternative, validated techniques are available, the frequency of testing may take account of a risk-benefit approach. The principle of bracketing and matrixing designs may be applied if scientifically justified in the protocol.

6.33 In certain situations, additional batches should be included in the on-going stability programme.

For example, an on-going stability study should be conducted after any significant change or significant deviation to the process or package. Any reworking, reprocessing or recovery operation should also be considered for inclusion.

6.34 Results of on-going stability studies should be made available to key personnel and, in particular, to the Qualified Person(s). Where on-going stability studies are carried out at a site other than the site of manufacture of the bulk or finished product, there should be a written agreement between the parties concerned. Results of on-going stability studies should be available at the site of manufacture for review by the competent authority.

6.35 Out of specification or significant atypical trends should be investigated. Any confirmed out of specification result, or significant negative trend, affecting product batches released on the market should be reported to the relevant competent authorities. The possible impact on batches on the market should be considered in accordance with Chapter 8 of the GMP Guide and in consultation with the relevant competent authorities.

6.36 A summary of all the data generated, including any interim conclusions on the programme, should be written and maintained. This summary should be subjected to periodic review.

Technical transfer of testing methods

6.37 Prior to transferring a test method, the transferring site should verify that the test method(s) comply with those as described in the Marketing Authorisation or the relevant technical dossier.
The original validation of the test method(s) should be reviewed to ensure compliance with current ICH/VICH requirements. A gap analysis should be performed and documented to identify any supplementary validation that should be performed, prior to commencing the technical transfer process.

6.38 The transfer of testing methods from one laboratory (transferring laboratory) to another laboratory (receiving laboratory) should be described in a detailed protocol.

6.39 The transfer protocol should include, but not be limited to, the following parameters:

i. Identification of the testing to be performed and the relevant test method(s) undergoing transfer;

ii. Identification of the additional training requirements;

iii. Identification of standards and samples to be tested;

iv. Identification of any special transport and storage conditions of test items;

v. The acceptance criteria which should be based upon the current validation study of the methodology and with respect to ICH/VICH requirements.

6.40 Deviations from the protocol should be investigated prior to closure of the technical transfer process. The technical transfer report should document the comparative outcome of the process and should identify areas requiring further test method revalidation, if applicable.

6.41 Where appropriate, specific requirements described in others European Guidelines, should be addressed for the transfer of particular testing methods (e.g Near Infrared Spectroscopy).

Notes

EudraLex

The Rules Governing Medicinal Products in the European Union

Volume 4

EU Guidelines for Good Manufacturing Practice for Medicinal Products for Human and Veterinary Use

Chapter 7

Outsourced Activities

Legal basis for publishing the detailed guidelines: Article 47 of Directive 2001/83/EC on the Community code relating to medicinal products for human use and Article 51 of Directive 2001/82/EC on the Community code relating to veterinary medicinal products. This document provides guidance for the interpretation of the principles and guidelines of good manufacturing practice (GMP) for medicinal products as laid down in Directive 2003/94/EC for medicinal products for human use and Directive 91/412/EEC for veterinary use.

Status of the document: revision 1

Reasons for changes: In view of the ICH Q10 guideline on the Pharmaceutical Quality System, Chapter 7 of the GMP Guide has been revised in order to provide updated guidance on outsourced GMP regulated activities beyond the current scope of contract manufacture and analysis operations. The title of the Chapter has been changed to reflect this.

Deadline for coming into operation: 31 January 2013

Principle

Any activity covered by the GMP Guide that is outsourced should be appropriately defined, agreed and controlled in order to avoid misunderstandings which could result in a product or operation of unsatisfactory quality. There must be a written Contract between the Contract Giver and the Contract Acceptor which clearly establishes the duties of each party. The Quality Management System of the Contract Giver must clearly state the way that the Qualified Person certifying each batch of product for release exercises his full responsibility.

Note: This Chapter deals with the responsibilities of manufacturers towards the Competent Authorities of the Member States with respect to the granting of marketing and manufacturing authorizations. It is not intended in any way to affect the respective liability of Contract Acceptors and Contract Givers to consumers; this is governed by other provisions of Community and national law.

General

7.1 There should be a written Contract covering the outsourced activities, the products or operations to which they are related, and any technical arrangements made in connection with it.

7.2 All arrangements for the outsourced activities including any proposed changes in technical or other arrangements should be in accordance with regulations in force, and the Marketing Authorisation for the product concerned, where applicable.

7.3 Where the marketing authorization holder and the manufacturer are not the same, appropriate arrangements should be in place, taking into account the principles described in this chapter.

The Contract Giver

7.4 The pharmaceutical quality system of the Contract Giver should include the control and review of any outsourced activities. The Contract Giver is ultimately responsible to ensure processes are in place to assure the control of outsourced activities. These processes should incorporate quality risk management principles and notably include:

7.5 Prior to outsourcing activities, the Contract Giver is responsible for assessing the legality, suitability and the competence of the Contract Acceptor to carry out successfully the outsourced activities. The Contract Giver is also responsible for ensuring by means of the Contract that the principles and guidelines of GMP as interpreted in this Guide are followed.

7.6 The Contract Giver should provide the Contract Acceptor with all the information and knowledge necessary to carry out the contracted operations correctly in accordance with regulations in force, and the Marketing Authorisation for the product concerned. The Contract Giver should ensure that the Contract Acceptor is fully aware of any problems associated with the product or the work which might pose a hazard to his premises, equipment, personnel, other materials or other products.

7.7 The Contract Giver should monitor and review the performance of the Contract Acceptor and the identification and implementation of any needed improvement.

7.8 The Contract Giver should be responsible for reviewing and assessing the records and the results related to the outsourced activities. He should also ensure, either by himself, or based on the confirmation of the Contract Acceptor's Qualified Person, that all products and materials delivered to him by the Contract Acceptor have been processed in accordance with GMP and the marketing authorisation.

The Contract Acceptor

7.9 The Contract Acceptor must be able to carry out satisfactorily the work ordered by the Contract Giver such as having adequate premises, equipment, knowledge, experience, and competent personnel.

7.10 The Contract Acceptor should ensure that all products, materials and knowledge delivered to him are suitable for their intended purpose.

7.11 The Contract Acceptor should not subcontract to a third party any of the work entrusted to him under the Contract without the Contract Giver's prior evaluation and approval of the arrangements. Arrangements made between the Contract Acceptor and any third party should ensure that information and knowledge, including those from assessments of the suitability of the third party, are made available in the same way as between the original Contract Giver and Contract Acceptor.

7.12 The Contract Acceptor should not make un authorized changes, outside the terms of the Contract, which may adversely affect the quality of the outsourced activities for the Contract Giver.

7.13 The Contract Acceptor should understand that outsourced activities, including contract analysis, may be subject to inspection by the competent authorities.

The Contract

7.14 A Contract should be drawn up between the Contract Giver and the Contract Acceptor which specifies their respective responsibilities and communication processes relating to the outsourced activities. Technical aspects of the Contract should be drawn up by competent persons suitably knowledgeable in related outsourced activities and Good Manufacturing Practice. All arrangements for outsourced activities must be in accordance with regulations in force and the Marketing Authorisation for the product concerned and agreed by both parties.

7.15 The Contract should describe clearly who undertakes each step of the outsourced activity, e.g. knowledge management, technology transfer, supply chain, subcontracting, quality and purchasing of materials, testing and releasing materials, undertaking production and quality controls (including in-process controls, sampling and analysis).

7.16 All records related to the outsourced activities, e.g. manufacturing, analytical and distribution records, and reference samples, should be kept by, or be available to, the Contract Giver. Any records relevant to assessing the quality of a product in the event of complaints or a suspected defect or to investigating in the case of a suspected falsified product must be accessible and specified in the relevant procedures of the Contract Giver.

7.17 The Contract should permit the Contract Giver to audit outsourced activities, performed by the Contract Acceptor or his mutually agreed sub contractors

EudraLex

The Rules Governing Medicinal Products in the European Union

Volume 4 EU Guidelines for Good Manufacturing Practice for Medicinal Products for Human and Veterinary Use

Part 1

Chapter 8: Complaints, Quality Defects and Product Recalls

Legal basis for publishing the detailed guidelines: Article 47 of Directive 2001/83/EC on the Community code relating to medicinal products for human use and Article 51 of Directive 2001/82/EC on the Community code relating to veterinary medicinal products. This document provides guidance for the interpretation of the principles and guidelines of good manufacturing practice (GMP) for medicinal products as laid down in Directive 2003/94/EC for medicinal products for human use and Directive 91/412/EEC for veterinary use.

Status of the document: Revision

Reasons for changes: Extensive changes have been made to this Chapter which now reflect that Quality Risk Management principles should be applied when investigating quality defects or complaints and when making decisions in relation to product recalls or other risk-mitigating actions. It emphasises the need for the cause(s) of quality defects or complaints to be investigated and determined, and that appropriate preventative actions are put in place to guard against a recurrence of the issue and clarifies expectations and responsibilities in relation to the reporting of quality defects to the Competent Authorities.

Deadline for coming into operation: 1 March 2015.

Principle

In order to protect public and animal health, a system and appropriate procedures should be in place to record, assess, investigate and review complaints including potential quality defects, and if necessary, to effectively and promptly recall medicinal products for human or veterinary use and investigational medicinal products from the distribution network. Quality Risk Management principles should be applied to the investigation and assessment of quality defects and to the decision-making process in relation to product recalls corrective and preventative actions and other risk-reducing actions. Guidance in relation to these principles is provided in Chapter 1.

All concerned competent authorities should be informed in a timely manner in case of a confirmed quality defect (faulty manufacture, product deterioration, detection of falsification, non-compliance with the marketing authorisation or product specification file, or any other serious quality problems) with a medicinal or investigational medicinal product which may result in the recall of the product or an abnormal restriction in the supply. In situations where product on the market is found to be non-compliant with the marketing authorisation, there is no requirement to notify concerned competent authorities provided the degree of non-compliance satisfies the Annex 16 restrictions regarding the handling of unplanned deviations.

In case of outsourced activities, a contract should describe the role and responsibilities of the manufacturer, the marketing authorisation holder and/or sponsor and any other relevant third parties in relation to assessment, decision-making, and dissemination of information and implementation of risk-reducing actions relating to a defective product. Guidance in relation to contracts is provided in Chapter 7. Such contracts should also address how to contact those responsible at each party for the management of quality defect and recall issues.

Personnel and Organisation

8.1 Appropriately trained and experienced personnel should be responsible for managing complaint and quality defect investigations and for deciding the measures to be taken to manage any potential risk(s) presented by those issues, including recalls. These persons should be independent of the sales and marketing organisation, unless otherwise justified. If these persons do not include the Qualified Person involved in the certification for release of the concerned batch or batches, the latter should be made formally aware of any investigations, any risk-reducing actions and any recall operations, in a timely manner.

8.2 Sufficient trained personnel and resources should be made available for the handling, assessment, investigation and review of complaints and quality defects and for implementing any risk-reducing actions. Sufficient trained personnel and resources should also be available for the management of interactions with competent authorities.

8.3 The use of inter-disciplinary teams should be considered, including appropriately trained Quality Management personnel.

8.4 In situations in which complaint and quality defect handling is managed centrally within an organisation, the relative roles and responsibilities of the concerned parties should be documented. Central management should not, however, result in delays in the investigation and management of the issue.

Procedures for handling and investigating complaints including possible quality defects

8.5 There should be written procedures describing the actions to be taken upon receipt of a complaint. All complaints should be documented and assessed to establish if they represent a potential quality defect or other issue.

8.6 Special attention should be given to establishing whether a complaint or suspected quality defect relates to falsification.

8.7 As not all complaints received by a company may represent actual quality defects, complaints which do not indicate a potential quality defect should be documented appropriately and communicated to the relevant group or person responsible for the investigation and management of complaints of that nature, such as suspected adverse events.

8.8 There should be procedures in place to facilitate a request to investigate the quality of a batch of a medicinal product in order to support an investigation into a reported suspected adverse event.

8.9 When a quality defect investigation is initiated, procedures should be in place to address at least the following:

i. The description of the reported quality defect.

ii. The determination of the extent of the quality defect. The checking or testing of reference and/or retention samples should be considered as part of this, and in certain cases, a review of the batch production record, the batch certification record and the batch distribution records (especially for temperature-sensitive products) should be performed.

iii. The need to request a sample, or the return, of the defective product from the complainant and, where a sample is provided, the need for an appropriate evaluation to be carried out.

iv. The assessment of the risk(s) posed by the quality defect, based on the severity and extent of the quality defect.

v. The decision-making process that is to be used concerning the potential need for risk-reducing actions to be taken in the distribution network, such as batch or product recalls, or other actions.

vi. The assessment of the impact that any recall action may have on the availability of the medicinal product to patients/animals in any affected market, and the need to notify the relevant authorities of such impact.

vii. The internal and external communications that should be made in relation to a quality defect and its investigation.

viii. The identification of the potential root cause(s) of the quality defect.

ix. The need for appropriate Corrective and Preventative Actions (CAPAs) to be identified and implemented for the issue, and for the assessment of the effectiveness of those CAPAs.

Investigation and Decision-making

8.10 The information reported in relation to possible quality defects should be recorded, including all the original details. The validity and extent of all reported quality defects should be documented and assessed in accordance with Quality Risk Management principles in order to support decisions regarding the degree of investigation and action taken.

8.11 If a quality defect is discovered or suspected in a batch, consideration should be given to checking other batches and in some cases other products, in order to determine whether they are also affected. In particular, other batches which may contain portions of the defective batch or defective components should be investigated.

8.12 Quality defect investigations should include a review of previous quality defect reports or any other relevant information for any indication of specific or recurring problems requiring attention and possibly further regulatory action.

8.13 The decisions that are made during and following quality defect investigations should reflect the level of risk that is presented by the quality defect as well as the seriousness of any non-compliance with respect to the requirements of the marketing authorisation/product specification file or GMP. Such decisions should be timely to ensure that patient and animal safety is maintained, in a way that is commensurate with the level of risk that is presented by those issues.

8.14 As comprehensive information on the nature and extent of the quality defect may not always be available at the early stages of an investigation, the decision-making processes should still ensure that appropriate risk-reducing actions are taken at an appropriate time-point during such investigations. All the decisions and measures taken as a result of a quality defect should be documented.

8.15 Quality defects should be reported in a timely manner by the manufacturer to the marketing authorisation holder/sponsor and all concerned Competent Authorities in cases where the quality defect may result in the recall of the product or in an abnormal restriction in the supply of the product.

Root Cause Analysis and Corrective and Preventative Actions

8.16 An appropriate level of root cause analysis work should be applied during the investigation of quality defects. In cases where the true root cause(s) of the quality defect cannot be determined, consideration should be given to identifying the most likely root cause(s) and to addressing those.

8.17 Where human error is suspected or identified as the cause of a quality defect, this should be formally justified and care should be exercised so as to ensure that process, procedural or system-based errors or problems are not overlooked, if present.

8.18 Appropriate CAPAs should be identified and taken in response to a quality defect. The effectiveness of such actions should be monitored and assessed.

8.19 Quality defect records should be reviewed and trend analyses should be performed regularly for any indication of specific or recurring problems requiring attention.

Product Recalls and other potential risk-reducing actions

8.20 There should be established written procedures, regularly reviewed and updated when necessary, in order to undertake any recall activity or implement any other risk-reducing actions.

8.21 After a product has been placed on the market, any retrieval of it from the distribution network as a result of a quality defect should be regarded and managed as a recall. (This provision does not apply to the retrieval (or return) of samples of the product from the distribution network to facilitate an investigation into a quality defect issue/report.)

8.22 Recall operations should be capable of being initiated promptly and at any time. In certain cases recall operations may need to be initiated to protect public or animal health prior to establishing the root cause(s) and full extent of the quality defect

8.23 The batch/product distribution records should be readily available to the persons responsible for recalls, and should contain sufficient information on wholesalers and directly supplied customers (with addresses, phone and/or fax numbers inside and outside working hours, batches and amounts delivered), including those for exported products and medical samples.

8.24 In the case of investigational medicinal products, all trial sites should be identified and the countries of destination should be indicated. In the case of an investigational medicinal product for which a marketing authorisation has been issued, the manufacturer of the investigational medicinal product should, in cooperation with the sponsor, inform the marketing authorisation holder of any quality defect that could be related to the authorised medicinal product. The sponsor should implement a procedure for the rapid unblinding of blinded products, where this is necessary for a prompt recall. The sponsor should ensure that the procedure discloses the identity of the blinded product only in so far as is necessary.

8.25 Consideration should be given following consultation with the concerned Competent Authorities, as to how far into the distribution network a recall action should extend, taking into account the potential risk to public or animal health and any impact that the proposed recall action may have. The Competent Authorities should also be informed in situations in which no recall action is being proposed for a defective batch because the batch has expired (such as with short shelf-life products.)

8.26 All concerned Competent Authorities should be informed in advance in cases where products are intended to be recalled. For very serious issues (i.e. those with the potential to seriously impact upon patient or animal health), rapid risk-reducing actions (such as a product recall) may have to be taken in advance of notifying the Competent Authorities. Wherever possible, attempts should be made to agree these in advance of their execution with the concerned Competent Authorities

8.27 It should also be considered whether the proposed recall action may affect different markets in different ways, and if this is the case, appropriate market-specific risk-reducing actions should be developed and discussed with the concerned competent authorities. Taking account of its therapeutic use the risk of shortage of a medicinal product which has no authorised alternative should be considered before deciding on a risk-reducing action such as a recall. Any decisions not to execute a risk-reducing action which would otherwise be required should be agreed with the competent authority in advance.

8.28 Recalled products should be identified and stored separately in a secure area while awaiting a decision on their fate. A formal disposition of all recalled batches should be made and documented. The rationale for any decision to rework recalled products should be documented and discussed with the relevant competent authority. The extent of shelf-life remaining for any reworked batches that are being considered for placement onto the market should also be considered.

8.29 The progress of the recall process should be recorded until closure and a final report issued, including a reconciliation between the delivered and recovered quantities of the concerned products/batches.

8.30 The effectiveness of the arrangements in place for recalls should be periodically evaluated to confirm that they remain robust and fit for use. Such evaluations should extend to both within office-hour situations as well as out-of-office hour situations and, when performing such evaluations, consideration should be given as to whether mock-recall actions should be performed. This evaluation should be documented and justified.

8.31 In addition to recalls, there are other potential risk-reducing actions that may be considered in order to manage the risks presented by quality defects. Such actions may include the issuance of cautionary communications to healthcare professionals in relation to their use of a batch that is potentially defective. These should be considered on a case-by-case basis and discussed with the concerned competent authorities.

Notes

CHAPTER 9 SELF INSPECTION

Principle

Self inspections should be conducted in order to monitor the implementation and compliance with Good Manufacturing Practice principles and to propose necessary corrective measures.

9.1
Personnel matters, premises, equipment, documentation, production, quality control, distribution of the medicinal products, arrangements for dealing with complaints and recalls, and self inspection, should be examined at intervals following a pre-arranged programme in order to verify their conformity with the principles of Quality Assurance.

9.2
Self inspections should be conducted in an independent and detailed way by designated competent person(s) from the company. Independent audits by external experts may also be useful.

9.3
All self inspections should be recorded. Reports should contain all the observations made during the inspections and, where applicable, proposals for corrective measures. Statements on the actions subsequently taken should also be recorded.

Notes

GLOSSARY

Definitions given below apply to the words as used in this guide. They may have different meanings in other contexts.

AIR-LOCK

An enclosed space with two or more doors, and which is interposed between two or more rooms, e.g. of differing class of cleanliness, for the purpose of controlling the air-flow between those rooms when they need to be entered. An air-lock is designed for and used by either people or goods.

BATCH (OR LOT)

A defined quantity of starting material, packaging material or product processed in one process or series of processes so that it could be expected to be homogeneous.

Note: To complete certain stages of manufacture, it may be necessary to divide a batch into a number of sub batches, which are later brought together to form a final homogeneous batch. In the case of continuous manufacture, the batch must correspond to a defined fraction of the production, characterised by its intended homogeneity.

For control of the finished product, the following definition has been given in Annex 1 of Directive 2001/83/EC as amended by Directive 2003/63/EC: 'For the control of the finished product, a batch of a proprietary medicinal product comprises all the units of a pharmaceutical form which are made from the same initial mass of material and have undergone a single series of manufacturing operations or a single sterilisation operation or, in the case of a continuous production process, all the units manufactured in a given period of time'.

BATCH NUMBER (OR LOT NUMBER)

A distinctive combination of numbers and/or letters which specifically identifies a batch.

BIOGENERATOR

A contained system, such as a fermenter, into which biological agents are introduced along with other materials so as to effect their multiplication or their production of other substances by reaction with the other materials. Biogenerators are generally fitted with devices for regulation, control, connection, material addition and material withdrawal.

BIOLOGICAL AGENTS

Micro-organisms, including genetically engineered micro-organisms, cell cultures and endoparasites, whether pathogenic or not.

BULK PRODUCT

Any product which has completed all processing stages up to, but not including, final packaging.

CALIBRATION

The set of operations which establish, under specified conditions, the relationship between values indicated by a measuring instrument or measuring system, or values represented by a material measure, and the corresponding known values of a reference standard.

CELL BANK

Cell bank system: A cell bank system is a system whereby successive batches of a product are manufactured by culture in cells derived from the same master cell bank. A number of containers from the master cell bank are used to prepare a working cell bank. The cell bank system is validated for a passage level or number of population doublings beyond that achieved during routine production.

Master cell bank: A culture of [fully characterised] cells distributed into containers in a single operation, processed together in such a manner as to ensure uniformity and stored in such a manner as to ensure stability. A master cell bank is usually stored at - 70°C or lower.

Working cell bank: A culture of cells derived from the master cell bank and intended for use in the preparation of production cell cultures. The working cell bank is usually stored at - 70°C or lower.

CELL CULTURE

The result from the in-vitro growth of cells isolated from multicellular organisms.

CLEAN AREA

An area with defined environmental control of particulate and microbial contamination, constructed and used in such a way as to reduce the introduction, generation and retention of contaminants within the area.

Note: The different degrees of environmental control are defined in the Supplementary Guidelines for the Manufacture of sterile medicinal products.

CLEAN/CONTAINED AREA

An area constructed and operated in such a manner that will achieve the aims of both a clean area and a contained area at the same time.

CONTAINMENT

The action of confining a biological agent or other entity within a defined space.

Primary containment: A system of containment which prevents the escape of a biological agent into the immediate working environment. It involves the use of closed containers or safety biological cabinets along with secure operating procedures.

Secondary containment: A system of containment which prevents the escape of a biological agent into the external environment or into other working areas. It involves the use of rooms with specially designed air handling, the existence of airlocks and/or sterilisers for the exit of materials and secure operating procedures. In many cases it may add to the effectiveness of primary containment.

CONTAINED AREA

An area constructed and operated in such a manner (and equipped with appropriate air handling and filtration) so as to prevent contamination of the external environment by biological agents from within the area.

CONTROLLED AREA

An area constructed and operated in such a manner that some attempt is made to control the introduction of potential contamination (an air supply approximating to grade D may be appropriate), and the consequences of accidental release of living organisms. The level of control exercised should reflect the nature of the organism employed in the process. At a minimum, the area should be maintained at a pressure negative to the immediate external environment and allow for the efficient removal of small quantities of airborne contaminants.

COMPUTERISED SYSTEM

A system including the input of data, electronic processing and the output of information to be used either for reporting or automatic control.

CROSS CONTAMINATION

Contamination of a material or of a product with another material or product.

CRUDE PLANT (VEGETABLE DRUG)

Fresh or dried medicinal plant or parts thereof.

CRYOGENIC VESSEL

A container designed to contain liquefied gas at extremely low temperature.

CYLINDER

A container designed to contain gas at a high pressure.

EXOTIC ORGANISM

A biological agent where either the corresponding disease does not exist in a given country or geographical area, or where the disease is the subject of prophylactic measures or an eradication programme undertaken in the given country or geographical area.

FINISHED PRODUCT

A medicinal product which has undergone all stages of production, including packaging in its final container.

HERBAL MEDICINAL PRODUCT

Medicinal product containing, as active ingredients, exclusively plant material and/or vegetable drug preparations.

INFECTED

Contaminated with extraneous biological agents and therefore capable of spreading infection.

IN-PROCESS CONTROL

Checks performed during production in order to monitor and if necessary to adjust the process to ensure that the product conforms its specification. The control of the environment or equipment may also be regarded as a part of in-process control.

INTERMEDIATE PRODUCT

Partly processed material which must undergo further manufacturing steps before it becomes a bulk product.

LIQUIFIABLE GASES

Those which, at the normal filling temperature and pressure, remain as a liquid in the cylinder.

MANIFOLD

Equipment or apparatus designed to enable one or more gas containers to be filled simultaneously from the same source.

MANUFACTURE

All operations of purchase of materials and products, Production, Quality Control, release, storage, distribution of medicinal products and the related controls.

MANUFACTURER

Holder of a Manufacturing Authorisation as described in Article 40 of Directive 2001/83/EC[1].

---

[1] Article 44 of Directive 2001/82/EC

MEDICINAL PLANT

Plant the whole or part of which is used for medicinal purpose.

MEDICINAL PRODUCT

Any substance or combination of substances presented for treating or preventing disease in human beings or animals.

Any substance or combination of substances which may be administered to human beings or animals with a view to making a medical diagnosis or to restoring, correcting or modifying physiological functions in human beings or in animals is likewise considered a medicinal product.

PACKAGING

All operations, including filling and labelling, which a bulk product has to undergo in order to become a finished product.

Note: Sterile filling would not normally be regarded as part of packaging, the bulk product being the filled, but not finally packaged, primary containers.

PACKAGING MATERIAL

Any material employed in the packaging of a medicinal product, excluding any outer packaging used for transportation or shipment. Packaging materials are referred to as primary or secondary according to whether or not they are intended to be in direct contact with the product.

PROCEDURES

Description of the operations to be carried out, the precautions to be taken and measures to be applied directly or indirectly related to the manufacture of a medicinal product.

PRODUCTION

All operations involved in the preparation of a medicinal product, from receipt of materials, through processing and packaging, to its completion as a finished product.

QUALIFICATION

Action of proving that any equipment works correctly and actually leads to the expected results. The word *validation* is sometimes widened to incorporate the concept of qualification.

QUALITY CONTROL

See Chapter 1.

QUARANTINE

The status of starting or packaging materials, intermediate, bulk or finished products isolated physically or by other effective means whilst awaiting a decision on their release or refusal.

RADIOPHARMACEUTICAL

"Radiopharmaceutical" shall mean any medicinal product which, when ready for use, contains one or more radionuclides (radioactive isotopes) included for a medicinal purpose (Article 1(6) of Directive 2001/83/EC.

RECONCILIATION

A comparison, making due allowance for normal variation, between the amount of product or materials theoretically and actually produced or used.

RECORD

See Chapter 4.

RECOVERY

The introduction of all or part of previous batches of the required quality into another batch at a defined stage of manufacture.

REPROCESSING

The reworking of all or part of a batch of product of an unacceptable quality from a defined stage of production so that its quality may be rendered acceptable by one or more additional operations.

RETURN

Sending back to the manufacturer or distributor of a medicinal product which may or may not present a quality defect.

SEED LOT

Seed lot system: A seed lot system is a system according to which successive batches of a product are derived from the same master seed lot at a given passage level. For routine production, a working seed lot is prepared from the master seed lot. The final product is derived from the working seed lot and has not undergone more passages from the master seed lot than the vaccine shown in clinical studies to be satisfactory with respect to safety and efficacy. The origin and the passage history of the master seed lot and the working seed lot are recorded.

Master seed lot: A culture of a micro-organism distributed from a single bulk into containers in a single operation in such a manner as to ensure uniformity, to prevent contamination and to ensure stability. A master seed lot in liquid form is usually stored at or below - 70°C. A freezedried master seed lot is stored at a temperature known to ensure stability.

Working seed lot: A culture of a micro-organism derived from the master seed lot and intended for use in production. Working seed lots are distributed into containers and stored as described above for master seed lots.

SPECIFICATION

See Chapter 4.

STARTING MATERIAL

Any substance used in the production of a medicinal product, but excluding packaging materials.

STERILITY

Sterility is the absence of living organisms. The conditions of the sterility test are given in the European Pharmacopoeia.

SYSTEM

Is used in the sense of a regulated pattern of interacting activities and techniques which are united to form an organised whole.

VALIDATION

Action of proving, in accordance with the principles of Good Manufacturing Practice, that any procedure, process, equipment, material, activity or system actually leads to the expected results (see also qualification).

Notes

Notes

ICH Q7

ICH
INTERNATIONAL CONFERENCE ON
HARMONISATION REGULATIONS

GOOD MANUFACTURING PRACTICE
GUIDE FOR ACTIVE
PHARMACEUTICAL INGREDIENTS

ICH Q7

Printed by GMP Publications, Inc.
Tel: 866-544-9007 or 856-810-7331
Fax: 866-544-9002
http://www.gmppublications.com
sales@gmppublications.com

INTERNATIONAL CONFERENCE ON HARMONISATION OF
TECHNICAL REQUIREMENTS FOR REGISTRATION OF
PHARMACEUTICALS FOR HUMAN USE

ICH HARMONISED TRIPARTITE GUIDELINE

GOOD MANUFACTURING PRACTICE GUIDE FOR ACTIVE PHARMACEUTICAL INGREDIENTS

Q7

Current *Step 4* version
dated 10 November 2000

This Guideline has been developed by the appropriate ICH Expert Working Group and has been subject to consultation by the regulatory parties, in accordance with the ICH Process. At Step 4 of the Process the final draft is recommended for adoption to the regulatory bodies of the European Union, Japan and USA.

Q7
Document History

First Codification	History	Date	New Codification November 2005
Q7A	Approval by the Steering Committee under *Step 2* and release for public consultation.	19 July 2000	Q7

Current *Step 4* version

Q7A	Approval by the Steering Committee under *Step 4* and recommendation for adoption to the three ICH regulatory bodies.	10 November 2000	Q7

GOOD MANUFACTURING PRACTICE GUIDE FOR ACTIVE PHARMACEUTICAL INGREDIENTS

ICH Harmonised Tripartite Guideline
Having reached *Step 4* of the ICH Process at the ICH Steering Committee meeting on 10 November 2000, this guideline is recommended

TABLE OF CONTENTS

1. **INTRODUCTION**
   1.1 Objective
   1.2 Regulatory Applicability
   1.3 Scope
2. **QUALITY MANAGEMENT**
   2.1 Principles
   2.2 Responsibilities of the Quality
   2.3 Responsibility for Production Activities
   2.4 Internal Audits (Self Inspection)
   2.5 Product Quality Review
3. **PERSONNEL**
   3.1 Personnel Qualifications
   3.2 Personnel Hygiene
   3.3 Consultants
4. **BUILDINGS AND**
   4.1 Design and Construction
   4.2 Utilities
   4.3 Water
   4.4 Containment
   4.5 Lighting
   4.6 Sewage and Refuse
   4.7 Sanitation and Maintenance
5. **PROCESS EQUIPMENT**
   5.1 Design and Construction
   5.2 Equipment Maintenance and Cleaning
   5.3 Calibration
   5.4 Computerized Systems
6. **DOCUMENTATION AND RECORDS**
   6.1 Documentation System and Specifications
   6.2 Equipment Cleaning and Use Record
   6.3 Records of Raw Materials, Intermediates, APIs Labelling and Packaging Materials

    6.4   Master Production Instructions (Master Production and Control Records)
    6.5   Batch Production Records (Batch Production and Control Records)
    6.6   Laboratory Control Records
    6.7   Batch Production Record Review

7.   MATERIALS MANAGEMENT
    7.1   General Controls
    7.2   Receipt and Quarantine
    7.3   Sampling and Testing of Incoming Production Materials
    7.4   Storage
    7.5   Re-evaluation

8.   PRODUCTION AND IN-PROCESS CONTROLS
    8.1   Production Operations
    8.2   Time Limits
    8.3   In-process Sampling and Controls
    8.4   Blending Batches of Intermediates or APIs
    8.5   Contamination Control

9.   PACKAGING AND IDENTIFICATION LABELLING OF APIs AND INTERMEDIATES
    9.1   General
    9.2   Packaging Materials
    9.3   Label Issuance and Control
    9.4   Packaging and Labelling Operations

10. STORAGE AND DISTRIBUTION
    10.1 Warehousing Procedures
    10.2 Distribution Procedures

11. LABORATORY CONTROLS
    11.1 General Controls
    11.2 Testing of Intermediates and APIs
    11.3 Validation of Analytical Procedures
    11.4 Certificates of Analysis
    11.5 Stability Monitoring of APIs
    11.6 Expiry and Retest Dating
    11.7 Reserve/Retention Samples

12. VALIDATION
    12.1 Validation Policy
    12.2 Validation Documentation
    12.3 Qualification
    12.4 Approaches to Process Validation
    12.5 Process Validation Program

- 12.6 Periodic Review of Validated Systems
- 12.7 Cleaning Validation
- 12.8 Validation of Analytical Methods
13. CHANGE CONTROL
14. REJECTION AND RE-USE OF MATERIALS
- 14.1 Rejection
- 14.2 Reprocessing
- 14.3 Reworking
- 14.4 Recovery of Materials and Solvents
- 14.5 Returns
15. COMPLAINTS AND RECALLS
16. CONTRACT MANUFACTURERS (INCLUDING LABORATORIES)
17. AGENTS, BROKERS, TRADERS, DISTRIBUTORS, REPACKERS, AND RELABELLERS
- 17.1 Applicability
- 17.2 Traceability of Distributed APIs and Intermediates
- 17.3 Quality Management
- 17.4 Repackaging, Relabelling and Holding of APIs and Intermediates
- 17.5 Stability
- 17.6 Transfer of Information
- 17.7 Handling of Complaints and Recalls
- 17.8 Handling of Returns
18. SPECIFIC GUIDANCE FOR APIs MANUFACTURED BY CELL CULTURE/FERMENTATION
- 18.1 General
- 18.2 Cell Bank Maintenance and Recordkeeping
- 18.3 Cell Culture/Fermentation
- 18.4 Harvesting, Isolation, and Purification
- 18.5 Viral Removal/Inactivation Steps
19. APIs FOR USE IN CLINICAL TRIALS
- 19.1 General
- 19.2 Quality
- 19.3 Equipment and Facilities
- 19.4 Control of Raw Materials
- 19.5 Production
- 19.6 Validation
- 19.7 Changes
- 19.8 Laboratory Controls
- 19.9 Documentation
20. GLOSSARY

GOOD MANUFACTURING PRACTICE GUIDE FOR ACTIVE PHARMACEUTICAL INGREDIENTS

1. INTRODUCTION

1.1 Objective

This document (Guide) is intended to provide guidance regarding good manufacturing practice (GMP) for the manufacturing of active pharmaceutical ingredients (APIs) under an appropriate system for managing quality. It is also intended to help ensure that APIs meet the requirements for quality and purity that they purport or are represented to possess.

In this Guide "manufacturing" is defined to include all operations of receipt of materials, production, packaging, repackaging, labelling, relabelling, quality control, release, storage and distribution of APIs and the related controls. In this Guide the term "should" indicates recommendations that are expected to apply unless shown to be inapplicable or replaced by an alternative demonstrated to provide at least an equivalent level of quality assurance. For the purposes of this Guide, the terms "current good manufacturing practices" and "good manufacturing practices" are equivalent.

The Guide as a whole does not cover safety aspects for the personnel engaged in the manufacture, nor aspects of protection of the environment. These controls are inherent responsibilities of the manufacturer and are governed by national laws.

This Guide is not intended to define registration/filing requirements or modify pharmacopoeial requirements. This Guide does not affect the ability of the responsible regulatory agency to establish specific registration/filing requirements regarding APIs within the context of marketing/manufacturing authorizations or drug applications. All commitments in registration/filing documents must be met.

1.2 Regulatory Applicability

Within the world community, materials may vary as to the legal classification as an API. When a material is classified as an API in the region or country in which it is manufactured or used in a drug product, it should be manufactured according to this Guide.

1.3 Scope

This Guide applies to the manufacture of APIs for use in human drug (medicinal) products. It applies to the manufacture of sterile APIs only up to the point immediately prior to the APIs being rendered sterile. The sterilization and aseptic processing of sterile APIs are not covered by this guidance, but should be performed in accordance with GMP guidelines for drug (medicinal) products as defined by local authorities.

This Guide covers APIs that are manufactured by chemical synthesis, extraction, cell culture/fermentation, by recovery from natural sources, or by any combination of these processes. Specific guidance for APIs manufactured by cell culture/fermentation is described in Section 18.

This Guide excludes all vaccines, whole cells, whole blood and plasma, blood and plasma derivatives (plasma fractionation), and gene therapy APIs. However, it does include APIs that are produced using blood or plasma as raw materials. Note that cell substrates (mammalian, plant, insect or microbial cells, tissue or animal sources including transgenic animals) and early process steps may be subject to GMP but are not covered by this Guide. In addition, the Guide does not apply to medical gases, bulk-packaged drug (medicinal) products, and manufacturing/control aspects specific to radiopharmaceuticals.

Section 19 contains guidance that only applies to the manufacture of APIs used in the production of drug (medicinal) products specifically for clinical trials (investigational medicinal products).

An "API Starting Material" is a raw material, intermediate, or an API that is used in the production of an API and that is incorporated as a significant structural fragment into the structure of the API. An API Starting Material can be an article of commerce, a material purchased from one or more suppliers under contract or commercial agreement, or produced in-house. API Starting Materials normally have defined chemical properties and structure.

The company should designate and document the rationale for the point at which production of the API begins. For synthetic processes, this is known as the point at which "API Starting Materials" are entered into the process. For other processes (e.g. fermentation, extraction, purification, etc) this rationale should be established on a case-by-case basis. Table 1 gives guidance on the point at which the API Starting Material is normally introduced into the process.

From this point on, appropriate GMP as defined in this Guide should be applied to these intermediate and/or API manufacturing steps. This would include the validation of critical process steps determined to impact the quality of the API. However, it should be noted that the fact that a company chooses to validate a process step does not necessarily define that step as critical.

The guidance in this document would normally be applied to the steps shown in gray in Table 1. It does not imply that all steps shown should be completed. The stringency of GMP in API manufacturing should increase as the process proceeds from early API steps to final steps, purification, and packaging. Physical processing of APIs, such as granulation, coating or physical manipulation of particle size (e.g. milling, micronizing), should be conducted at least to the standards of this Guide.

This GMP Guide does not apply to steps prior to the introduction of the defined "API Starting Material".

Table 1: Application of this Guide to API Manufacturing

Type of Manufacturing	Application of this Guide to steps (shown in grey) used in this type of manufacturing				
Chemical Manufacturing	Production of the API Starting Material	Introduction of the API Starting Material into process	Production of Intermediate(s)	Isolation and purification	Physical processing, and packaging
API derived from animal sources	Collection of organ, fluid, or tissue	Cutting, mixing, and/or initial processing	Introduction of the API Starting Material into process	Isolation and purification	Physical processing, and packaging
API extracted from plant sources	Collection of plants	Cutting and initial extraction(s)	Introduction of the API Starting Material into process	Isolation and purification	Physical processing, and packaging
Herbal extracts used as API	Collection of plants	Cutting and initial extraction(s)		Further extraction	Physical processing, and packaging
API consisting of comminuted or powdered herbs	Collection of plants and/or cultivation and harvesting	Cutting/comminuting			Physical processing, and packaging
Biotechnology: fermentation/ cell culture	Establishment of master cell bank and working cell bank	Maintenance of working cell bank	Cell culture and/or fermentation	Isolation and purification	Physical processing, and packaging
"Classical" Fermentation to produce an API	Establishment of cell bank	Maintenance of the cell bank	Introduction of the cells into fermentation	Isolation and purification	Physical processing, and packaging

Increasing GMP Requirements →

2. QUALITY MANAGEMENT

2.1 Principles

2.10 Quality should be the responsibility of all persons involved in manufacturing.

2.11 Each manufacturer should establish, document, and implement an effective system for managing quality that involves the active participation of management and appropriate manufacturing personnel.

2.12 The system for managing quality should encompass the organisational structure, procedures, processes and resources, as well as activities necessary to ensure confidence that the API will meet its intended specifications for quality and purity. All quality related activities should be defined and documented.

2.13 There should be a quality unit(s) that is independent of production and that fulfills both quality assurance (QA) and quality control (QC) responsibilities. This can be in the form of separate QA and QC units or a single individual or group, depending upon the size and structure of the organization.

2.14 The persons authorised to release intermediates and APIs should be specified.

2.15 All quality related activities should be recorded at the time they are performed.

2.16 Any deviation from established procedures should be documented and explained.
Critical deviations should be investigated, and the investigation and its conclusions should be documented.

2.17 No materials should be released or used before the satisfactory completion of evaluation by the quality unit(s) unless there are appropriate systems in place to allow for such use (e.g. release under quarantine as described in Section 10.20 or the use of raw materials or intermediates pending completion of evaluation).

2.18 Procedures should exist for notifying responsible management in a timely manner of regulatory inspections, serious GMP deficiencies, product defects and related actions (e.g. quality related complaints, recalls, regulatory actions, etc.).

2.2 Responsibilities of the Quality Unit(s)

2.20 The quality unit(s) should be involved in all quality-related matters.

2.21 The quality unit(s) should review and approve all appropriate quality-related documents.

2.22 The main responsibilities of the independent quality unit(s) should not be delegated. These responsibilities should be described in writing and should include but not necessarily be limited to:

1. Releasing or rejecting all APIs. Releasing or rejecting intermediates for use outside the control of the manufacturing company;
2. Establishing a system to release or reject raw materials, intermediates, packaging and labelling materials;
3. Reviewing completed batch production and laboratory control records of critical process steps before release of the API for distribution;
4. Making sure that critical deviations are investigated and resolved;
5. Approving all specifications and master production instructions;
6. Approving all procedures impacting the quality of intermediates or APIs;
7. Making sure that internal audits (self-inspections) are performed;
8. Approving intermediate and API contract manufacturers;
9. Approving changes that potentially impact intermediate or API quality;
10. Reviewing and approving validation protocols and reports;
11. Making sure that quality related complaints are investigated and resolved;
12. Making sure that effective systems are used for maintaining and calibrating critical equipment;
13. Making sure that materials are appropriately tested and the results are reported;
14. Making sure that there is stability data to support retest or expiry dates and storage conditions on APIs and/or intermediates where appropriate; and
15. Performing product quality reviews (as defined in Section 2.5).

2.3 Responsibility for Production Activities

The responsibility for production activities should be described in writing, and should include but not necessarily be limited to:

1. Preparing, reviewing, approving and distributing the instructions for the production of intermediates or APIs according to written procedures;
2. Producing APIs and, when appropriate, intermediates according to pre-approved instructions;
3. Reviewing all production batch records and ensuring that these are completed and signed;

4. Making sure that all production deviations are reported and evaluated and that critical deviations are investigated and the conclusions are recorded;

5. Making sure that production facilities are clean and when appropriate disinfected;

6. Making sure that the necessary calibrations are performed and records kept;

7. Making sure that the premises and equipment are maintained and records kept;

8. Making sure that validation protocols and reports are reviewed and approved;

9. Evaluating proposed changes in product, process or equipment; and

10. Making sure that new and, when appropriate, modified facilities and equipment are qualified.

2.4 Internal Audits (Self Inspection)

2.40 In order to verify compliance with the principles of GMP for APIs, regular internal audits should be performed in accordance with an approved schedule.

2.41 Audit findings and corrective actions should be documented and brought to the attention of responsible management of the firm. Agreed corrective actions should be completed in a timely and effective manner.

2.5 Product Quality Review

2.50 Regular quality reviews of APIs should be conducted with the objective of verifying the consistency of the process. Such reviews should normally be conducted and documented annually and should include at least:
- A review of critical in-process control and critical API test results;
- A review of all batches that failed to meet established specification(s);
- A review of all critical deviations or non-conformances and related investigations;
- A review of any changes carried out to the processes or analytical methods;
- A review of results of the stability monitoring program;
- A review of all quality-related returns, complaints and recalls; and
- A review of adequacy of corrective actions.

2.51 The results of this review should be evaluated and an assessment made of whether corrective action or any revalidation should be undertaken. Reasons for such corrective action should be documented. Agreed corrective actions should be completed in a timely and effective manner.

3. PERSONNEL

3.1 Personnel Qualifications

3.10 There should be an adequate number of personnel qualified by appropriate education, training and/or experience to perform and supervise the manufacture of intermediates and APIs.

3.11 The responsibilities of all personnel engaged in the manufacture of intermediates and APIs should be specified in writing.

3.12 Training should be regularly conducted by qualified individuals and should cover, at a minimum, the particular operations that the employee performs and GMP as it relates to the employee's functions. Records of training should be maintained. Training should be periodically assessed.

3.2 Personnel Hygiene

3.20 Personnel should practice good sanitation and health habits.

3.21 Personnel should wear clean clothing suitable for the manufacturing activity with which they are involved and this clothing should be changed when appropriate. Additional protective apparel, such as head, face, hand, and arm coverings, should be worn when necessary, to protect intermediates and APIs from contamination.

3.22 Personnel should avoid direct contact with intermediates or APIs.

3.23 Smoking, eating, drinking, chewing and the storage of food should be restricted to certain designated areas separate from the manufacturing areas.

3.24 Personnel suffering from an infectious disease or having open lesions on the exposed surface of the body should not engage in activities that could result in compromising the quality of APIs. Any person shown at any time (either by medical examination or supervisory observation) to have an apparent illness or open lesions should be excluded from activities where the health condition could adversely affect the quality of the APIs until the condition is corrected or qualified medical personnel determine that the person's inclusion would not jeopardize the safety or quality of the APIs.

3.3 Consultants

3.30 Consultants advising on the manufacture and control of intermediates or APIs should have sufficient education, training, and experience, or any combination thereof, to advise on the subject for which they are retained.

3.31 Records should be maintained stating the name, address, qualifications, and type of service provided by these consultants.

4. BUILDINGS AND FACILITIES

4.1 Design and Construction

4.10 Buildings and facilities used in the manufacture of intermediates and APIs should be located, designed, and constructed to facilitate cleaning, maintenance, and operations as appropriate to the type and stage of manufacture. Facilities should also be designed to minimize potential contamination. Where microbiological specifications have been established for the intermediate or API, facilities should also be designed to limit exposure to objectionable microbiological contaminants as appropriate.

4.11 Buildings and facilities should have adequate space for the orderly placement of equipment and materials to prevent mix-ups and contamination.

4.12 Where the equipment itself (e.g., closed or contained systems) provides adequate protection of the material, such equipment can be located outdoors.

4.13 The flow of materials and personnel through the building or facilities should be designed to prevent mix-ups or contamination.

4.14 There should be defined areas or other control systems for the following activities:
- Receipt, identification, sampling, and quarantine of incoming materials, pending release or rejection;
- Quarantine before release or rejection of intermediates and APIs;
- Sampling of intermediates and APIs;
- Holding rejected materials before further disposition (e.g., return, reprocessing or destruction);
- Storage of released materials;
- Production operations;
- Packaging and labelling operations; and
- Laboratory operations.

4.15 Adequate, clean washing and toilet facilities should be provided for personnel. These washing facilities should be equipped with hot and cold water as appropriate, soap or detergent, air driers or single service towels. The washing and toilet facilities should be separate from, but easily accessible to, manufacturing areas. Adequate facilities for showering and/or changing clothes should be provided, when appropriate.

4.16 Laboratory areas/operations should normally be separated from production areas. Some laboratory areas, in particular those used for in-process controls, can be located in production areas, provided the operations of the production process do not adversely affect the accuracy of the laboratory measurements, and the laboratory and its operations do not adversely affect the production process or intermediate or API.

4.2   Utilities

4.20 All utilities that could impact on product quality (e.g. steam, gases, compressed air, and heating, ventilation and air conditioning) should be qualified and appropriately monitored and action should be taken when limits are exceeded. Drawings for these utility systems should be available.

4.21 Adequate ventilation, air filtration and exhaust systems should be provided, where appropriate. These systems should be designed and constructed to minimise risks of contamination and cross-contamination and should include equipment for control of air pressure, microorganisms (if appropriate), dust, humidity, and temperature, as appropriate to the stage of manufacture. Particular attention should be given to areas where APIs are exposed to the environment.

4.22 If air is recirculated to production areas, appropriate measures should be taken to control risks of contamination and cross-contamination.

4.23 Permanently installed pipework should be appropriately identified. This can be accomplished by identifying individual lines, documentation, computer control systems, or alternative means. Pipework should be located to avoid risks of contamination of the intermediate or API.

4.24 Drains should be of adequate size and should be provided with an air break or a suitable device to prevent back-siphonage, when appropriate.

4.3   Water

4.30 Water used in the manufacture of APIs should be demonstrated to be suitable for its intended use.

4.31 Unless otherwise justified, process water should, at a minimum, meet World Health Organization (WHO) guidelines for drinking (potable) water quality.

4.32 If drinking (potable) water is insufficient to assure API quality, and tighter chemical and/or microbiological water quality specifications are called for, appropriate specifications for physical/chemical attributes, total microbial counts, objectionable organisms and/or endotoxins should be established.

4.33 Where water used in the process is treated by the manufacturer to achieve a defined quality, the treatment process should be validated and monitored with appropriate action limits.

4.34 Where the manufacturer of a non-sterile API either intends or claims that it is suitable for use in further processing to produce a sterile drug (medicinal) product, water used in the final isolation and purification steps should be monitored and controlled for total microbial counts, objectionable organisms, and endotoxins.

4.4 Containment

4.40 Dedicated production areas, which can include facilities, air handling equipment and/or process equipment, should be employed in the production of highly sensitizing materials, such as penicillins or cephalosporins.

4.41 Dedicated production areas should also be considered when material of an infectious nature or high pharmacological activity or toxicity is involved (e.g., certain steroids or cytotoxic anti-cancer agents) unless validated inactivation and/or cleaning procedures are established and maintained.

4.42 Appropriate measures should be established and implemented to prevent cross-contamination from personnel, materials, etc. moving from one dedicated area to another.

4.43 Any production activities (including weighing, milling, or packaging) of highly toxic non-pharmaceutical materials such as herbicides and pesticides should not be conducted using the buildings and/or equipment being used for the production of APIs. Handling and storage of these highly toxic non-pharmaceutical materials should be separate from APIs.

4.5 Lighting

4.50 Adequate lighting should be provided in all areas to facilitate cleaning, maintenance, and proper operations.

4.6 Sewage and Refuse

4.60 Sewage, refuse, and other waste (e.g., solids, liquids, or gaseous by-products from manufacturing) in and from buildings and the immediate surrounding area should be disposed of in a safe, timely, and sanitary manner. Containers and/or pipes for waste material should be clearly identified.

4.7 Sanitation and Maintenance

4.70 Buildings used in the manufacture of intermediates and APIs should be properly maintained and repaired and kept in a clean condition.

4.71 Written procedures should be established assigning responsibility for sanitation and describing the cleaning schedules, methods, equipment, and materials to be used in cleaning buildings and facilities.

4.72 When necessary, written procedures should also be established for the use of suitable rodenticides, insecticides, fungicides, fumigating agents, and cleaning and sanitizing agents to prevent the contamination of equipment, raw materials, packaging/labelling materials, intermediates, and APIs.

5. PROCESS EQUIPMENT
5.1 Design and Construction

5.10 Equipment used in the manufacture of intermediates and APIs should be of appropriate design and adequate size, and suitably located for its intended use, cleaning, sanitization (where appropriate), and maintenance.

5.11 Equipment should be constructed so that surfaces that contact raw materials, intermediates, or APIs do not alter the quality of the intermediates and APIs beyond the official or other established specifications.

5.12 Production equipment should only be used within its qualified operating range.

5.13 Major equipment (e.g., reactors, storage containers) and permanently installed processing lines used during the production of an intermediate or API should be appropriately identified.

5.14 Any substances associated with the operation of equipment, such as lubricants, heating fluids or coolants, should not contact intermediates or APIs so as to alter their quality beyond the official or other established specifications. Any deviations from this should be evaluated to ensure that there are no detrimental effects upon the fitness for purpose of the material. Wherever possible, food grade lubricants and oils should be used.

5.15 Closed or contained equipment should be used whenever appropriate. Where open equipment is used, or equipment is opened, appropriate precautions should be taken to minimize the risk of contamination.

5.16 A set of current drawings should be maintained for equipment and critical installations (e.g., instrumentation and utility systems).

5.2 Equipment Maintenance and Cleaning

5.20 Schedules and procedures (including assignment of responsibility) should be established for the preventative maintenance of equipment.

5.21 Written procedures should be established for cleaning of equipment and its subsequent release for use in the manufacture of intermediates and APIs. Cleaning procedures should contain sufficient details to enable operators to clean each type of equipment in a reproducible and effective manner. These procedures should include:

- Assignment of responsibility for cleaning of equipment;
- Cleaning schedules, including, where appropriate, sanitizing schedules;
- A complete description of the methods and materials, including dilution of cleaning agents used to clean equipment;

- When appropriate, instructions for disassembling and reassembling each article of equipment to ensure proper cleaning;
- Instructions for the removal or obliteration of previous batch identification;
- Instructions for the protection of clean equipment from contamination prior to use;
- Inspection of equipment for cleanliness immediately before use, if practical; and
- Establishing the maximum time that may elapse between the completion of processing and equipment cleaning, when appropriate.

5.22 Equipment and utensils should be cleaned, stored, and, where appropriate, sanitized or sterilized to prevent contamination or carry-over of a material that would alter the quality of the intermediate or API beyond the official or other established specifications.

5.23 Where equipment is assigned to continuous production or campaign production of successive batches of the same intermediate or API, equipment should be cleaned at appropriate intervals to prevent build-up and carry-over of contaminants (e.g. degradants or objectionable levels of micro-organisms).

5.24 Non-dedicated equipment should be cleaned between production of different materials to prevent cross-contamination.

5.25 Acceptance criteria for residues and the choice of cleaning procedures and cleaning agents should be defined and justified.

5.26 Equipment should be identified as to its contents and its cleanliness status by appropriate means.

5.3 Calibration

5.30 Control, weighing, measuring, monitoring and test equipment that is critical for assuring the quality of intermediates or APIs should be calibrated according to written procedures and an established schedule.

5.31 Equipment calibrations should be performed using standards traceable to certified standards, if existing.

5.32 Records of these calibrations should be maintained.

5.33 The current calibration status of critical equipment should be known and verifiable.

5.34 Instruments that do not meet calibration criteria should not be used.

5.35 Deviations from approved standards of calibration on critical instruments should be investigated to determine if these could have had an impact on the quality of the intermediate(s) or API(s) manufactured using this equipment since the last successful calibration.

5.4 Computerized Systems

5.40 GMP related computerized systems should be validated. The depth and scope of validation depends on the diversity, complexity and criticality of the computerized application.

5.41 Appropriate installation qualification and operational qualification should demonstrate the suitability of computer hardware and software to perform assigned tasks.

5.42 Commercially available software that has been qualified does not require the same level of testing. If an existing system was not validated at time of installation, a retrospective validation could be conducted if appropriate documentation is available.

5.43 Computerized systems should have sufficient controls to prevent unauthorized access or changes to data. There should be controls to prevent omissions in data (e.g. system turned off and data not captured). There should be a record of any data change made, the previous entry, who made the change, and when the change was made.

5.44 Written procedures should be available for the operation and maintenance of computerized systems.

5.45 Where critical data are being entered manually, there should be an additional check on the accuracy of the entry. This can be done by a second operator or by the system itself.

5.46 Incidents related to computerized systems that could affect the quality of intermediates or APIs or the reliability of records or test results should be recorded and investigated.

5.47 Changes to the computerized system should be made according to a change procedure and should be formally authorized, documented and tested. Records should be kept of all changes, including modifications and enhancements made to the hardware, software and any other critical component of the system. These records should demonstrate that the system is maintained in a validated state.

5.48 If system breakdowns or failures would result in the permanent loss of records, a back-up system should be provided. A means of ensuring data protection should be established for all computerized systems.

5.49 Data can be recorded by a second means in addition to the computer system.

6. DOCUMENTATION AND RECORDS

6.1 Documentation System and Specifications

6.10 All documents related to the manufacture of intermediates or APIs should be prepared, reviewed, approved and distributed according to written procedures. Such documents can be in paper or electronic form.

6.11 The issuance, revision, superseding and withdrawal of all documents should be controlled with maintenance of revision histories.

6.12 A procedure should be established for retaining all appropriate documents (e.g., development history reports, scale-up reports, technical transfer reports, process validation reports, training records, production records, control records, and distribution records). The retention periods for these documents should be specified.

6.13 All production, control, and distribution records should be retained for at least 1 year after the expiry date of the batch. For APIs with retest dates, records should be retained for at least 3 years after the batch is completely distributed.

6.14 When entries are made in records, these should be made indelibly in spaces provided for such entries, directly after performing the activities, and should identify the person making the entry. Corrections to entries should be dated and signed and leave the original entry still readable.

6.15 During the retention period, originals or copies of records should be readily available at the establishment where the activities described in such records occurred. Records that can be promptly retrieved from another location by electronic or other means are acceptable.

6.16 Specifications, instructions, procedures, and records can be retained either as originals or as true copies such as photocopies, microfilm, microfiche, or other accurate reproductions of the original records. Where reduction techniques such as microfilming or electronic records are used, suitable retrieval equipment and a means to produce a hard copy should be readily available.

6.17 Specifications should be established and documented for raw materials, intermediates where necessary, APIs, and labelling and packaging materials. In addition, specifications may be appropriate for certain other materials, such as process aids, gaskets, or other materials used during the production of intermediates or APIs that could critically impact on quality. Acceptance criteria should be established and documented for in-process controls.

6.18 If electronic signatures are used on documents, they should be authenticated and secure.

6.2 Equipment Cleaning and Use Record

6.20 Records of major equipment use, cleaning, sanitization and/or sterilization and maintenance should show the date, time (if appropriate), product, and batch number of each batch processed in the equipment, and the person who performed the cleaning and maintenance.

6.21 If equipment is dedicated to manufacturing one intermediate or API, then individual equipment records are not necessary if batches of the intermediate or API follow in traceable sequence. In cases where dedicated equipment is employed, the records of cleaning, maintenance, and use can be part of the batch record or maintained separately.

6.3 Records of Raw Materials, Intermediates, API Labelling and Packaging Materials

6.30 Records should be maintained including:
- The name of the manufacturer, identity and quantity of each shipment of each batch of raw materials, intermediates or labelling and packaging materials for API's; the name of the supplier; the supplier's control number(s), if known, or other identification number; the number allocated on receipt; and the date of receipt;
- The results of any test or examination performed and the conclusions derived from this;
- Records tracing the use of materials;
- Documentation of the examination and review of API labelling and packaging materials for conformity with established specifications; and
- The final decision regarding rejected raw materials, intermediates or API labelling and packaging materials.

6.31 Master (approved) labels should be maintained for comparison to issued labels.

6.4 Master Production Instructions (Master Production and Control Records)

6.40 To ensure uniformity from batch to batch, master production instructions for each intermediate and API should be prepared, dated, and signed by one person and independently checked, dated, and signed by a person in the quality unit(s).

6.41 Master production instructions should include:
- The name of the intermediate or API being manufactured and an identifying document reference code, if applicable;
- A complete list of raw materials and intermediates designated by names or codes sufficiently specific to identify any special quality characteristics;
- An accurate statement of the quantity or ratio of each raw material or intermediate to be used, including the unit of measure. Where the quantity is not fixed, the calculation for each batch size or rate of production should be included. Variations to quantities should be included where they are justified;
- The production location and major production equipment to be used;
- Detailed production instructions, including the:
- sequences to be followed,
- ranges of process parameters to be used,

- sampling instructions and in-process controls with their acceptance criteria, where appropriate;
- time limits for completion of individual processing steps and/or the total process, where appropriate; and
- expected yield ranges at appropriate phases of processing or time;
- Where appropriate, special notations and precautions to be followed, or cross-references to these; and
- The instructions for storage of the intermediate or API to assure its suitability for use, including the labelling and packaging materials and special storage conditions with time limits, where appropriate.

6.5 Batch Production Records (Batch Production and Control Records)

6.50 Batch production records should be prepared for each intermediate and API and should include complete information relating to the production and control of each batch. The batch production record should be checked before issuance to assure that it is the correct version and a legible accurate reproduction of the appropriate master production instruction. If the batch production record is produced from a separate part of the master document, that document should include a reference to the current master production instruction being used.

6.51 These records should be numbered with a unique batch or identification number, dated and signed when issued. In continuous production, the product code together with the date and time can serve as the unique identifier until the final number is allocated.

6.52 Documentation of completion of each significant step in the batch production records (batch production and control records) should include:
- Dates and, when appropriate, times;
- Identity of major equipment (e.g., reactors, driers, mills, etc.) used;
- Specific identification of each batch, including weights, measures, and batch numbers of raw materials, intermediates, or any reprocessed materials used during manufacturing;
- Actual results recorded for critical process parameters;
- Any sampling performed;
- Signatures of the persons performing and directly supervising or checking each critical step in the operation;
- In-process and laboratory test results;
- Actual yield at appropriate phases or times;
- Description of packaging and label for intermediate or API;
- Representative label of API or intermediate if made commercially available;

- Any deviation noted, its evaluation, investigation conducted (if appropriate) or reference to that investigation if stored separately; and
- Results of release testing.

6.53 Written procedures should be established and followed for investigating critical deviations or the failure of a batch of intermediate or API to meet specifications.
The investigation should extend to other batches that may have been associated with the specific failure or deviation.

6.6 Laboratory Control Records

6.60 Laboratory control records should include complete data derived from all tests conducted to ensure compliance with established specifications and standards, including examinations and assays, as follows:
- A description of samples received for testing, including the material name or source, batch number or other distinctive code, date sample was taken, and, where appropriate, the quantity and date the sample was received for testing;
- A statement of or reference to each test method used;
- A statement of the weight or measure of sample used for each test as described by the method; data on or cross-reference to the preparation and testing of reference standards, reagents and standard solutions;
- A complete record of all raw data generated during each test, in addition to graphs, charts, and spectra from laboratory instrumentation, properly identified to show the specific material and batch tested;
- A record of all calculations performed in connection with the test, including, for example, units of measure, conversion factors, and equivalency factors;
- A statement of the test results and how they compare with established acceptance criteria;
- The signature of the person who performed each test and the date(s) the tests were performed; and
- The date and signature of a second person showing that the original records have been reviewed for accuracy, completeness, and compliance with established standards.

6.61 Complete records should also be maintained for:
- Any modifications to an established analytical method;
- Periodic calibration of laboratory instruments, apparatus, gauges, and recording devices;
- All stability testing performed on APIs; and
- Out-of-specification (OOS) investigations.

6.7 Batch Production Record Review

6.70 Written procedures should be established and followed for the review and approval of batch production and laboratory control records, including packaging and labelling, to determine compliance of the intermediate or API with established specifications before a batch is released or distributed.

6.71 Batch production and laboratory control records of critical process steps should be reviewed and approved by the quality unit(s) before an API batch is released or distributed. Production and laboratory control records of non-critical process steps can be reviewed by qualified production personnel or other units following procedures approved by the quality unit(s).

6.72 All deviation, investigation, and OOS reports should be reviewed as part of the batch record review before the batch is released.

6.73 The quality unit(s) can delegate to the production unit the responsibility and authority for release of intermediates, except for those shipped outside the control of the manufacturing company.

7. MATERIALS MANAGEMENT

7.1 General Controls

7.10 There should be written procedures describing the receipt, identification, quarantine, storage, handling, sampling, testing, and approval or rejection of materials.

7.11 Manufacturers of intermediates and/or APIs should have a system for evaluating the suppliers of critical materials.

7.12 Materials should be purchased against an agreed specification, from a supplier or suppliers approved by the quality unit(s).

7.13 If the supplier of a critical material is not the manufacturer of that material, the name and address of that manufacturer should be known by the intermediate and/or API manufacturer.

7.14 Changing the source of supply of critical raw materials should be treated according to Section 13, Change Control.

7.2 Receipt and Quarantine

7.20 Upon receipt and before acceptance, each container or grouping of containers of materials should be examined visually for correct labelling (including correlation between the name used by the supplier and the in-house name, if these are different), container damage, broken seals and evidence of tampering or contamination. Materials should be held under quarantine until they have been sampled, examined or tested as appropriate, and released for use.

7.21 Before incoming materials are mixed with existing stocks (e.g., solvents or stocks in silos), they should be identified as correct, tested, if appropriate, and released. Procedures should be available to prevent discharging incoming materialswrongly into the existing stock.

7.22 If bulk deliveries are made in non-dedicated tankers, there should be assurance of no cross-contamination from the tanker. Means of providing this assurance could include one or more of the following:
- certificate of cleaning
- testing for trace impurities
- audit of the supplier.

7.23 Large storage containers, and their attendant manifolds, filling and discharge lines should be appropriately identified.

7.24 Each container or grouping of containers (batches) of materials should be assigned and identified with a distinctive code, batch, or receipt number. This number should be used in recording the disposition of each batch. A system should be in place to identify the status of each batch.

7.3 Sampling and Testing of Incoming Production Materials

7.30 At least one test to verify the identity of each batch of material should be conducted, with the exception of the materials described below in 7.32. A supplier's Certificate of Analysis can be used in place of performing other tests, provided that the manufacturer has a system in place to evaluate suppliers.

7.31 Supplier approval should include an evaluation that provides adequate evidence (e.g., past quality history) that the manufacturer can consistently provide material meeting specifications. Full analyses should be conducted on at least three batches before reducing in-house testing. However, as a minimum, a full analysis should be performed at appropriate intervals and compared with the Certificates of Analysis. Reliability of Certificates of Analysis should be checked at regular intervals.

7.32 Processing aids, hazardous or highly toxic raw materials, other special materials, or materials transferred to another unit within the company's control do not need to be tested if the manufacturer's Certificate of Analysis is obtained, showing that these raw materials conform to established specifications. Visual examination of containers, labels, and recording of batch numbers should help in establishing the identity of these materials. The lack of on-site testing for these materials should be justified and documented.

7.33 Samples should be representative of the batch of material from which they are taken. Sampling methods should specify the number of containers to be sampled, which part of the container to sample, and the amount of material to be taken from each container. The number of containers to sample and the sample size should be based upon a sampling plan that takes into consideration the criticality of the material, material variability, past quality history of the supplier, and the quantity needed for analysis.

7.34 Sampling should be conducted at defined locations and by procedures designed to prevent contamination of the material sampled and contamination of other materials.

7.35 Containers from which samples are withdrawn should be opened carefully and subsequently reclosed. They should be marked to indicate that a sample has been taken.

7.4 Storage

7.40 Materials should be handled and stored in a manner to prevent degradation, contamination, and cross-contamination.

7.41 Materials stored in fiber drums, bags, or boxes should be stored off the floor and, when appropriate, suitably spaced to permit cleaning and inspection.

7.42 Materials should be stored under conditions and for a period that have no adverse affect on their quality, and should normally be controlled so that the oldest stock is used first.

7.43 Certain materials in suitable containers can be stored outdoors, provided identifying labels remain legible and containers are appropriately cleaned before opening and use.

7.44 Rejected materials should be identified and controlled under a quarantine system designed to prevent their unauthorised use in manufacturing.

7.5 Re-evaluation

7.50 Materials should be re-evaluated as appropriate to determine their suitability for use (e.g., after prolonged storage or exposure to heat or humidity).

8.   PRODUCTION AND IN-PROCESS CONTROLS

8.1 Production Operations

8.10 Raw materials for intermediate and API manufacturing should be weighed or measured under appropriate conditions that do not affect their suitability for use. Weighing and measuring devices should be of suitable accuracy for the intended use.

8.11 If a material is subdivided for later use in production operations, the container receiving the material should be suitable and should be so identified that the following information is available:
  - Material name and/or item code;

- Receiving or control number;
- Weight or measure of material in the new container; and
- Re-evaluation or retest date if appropriate.

8.12 Critical weighing, measuring, or subdividing operations should be witnessed or subjected to an equivalent control. Prior to use, production personnel should verify that the materials are those specified in the batch record for the intended intermediate or API.

8.13 Other critical activities should be witnessed or subjected to an equivalent control.

8.14 Actual yields should be compared with expected yields at designated steps in the production process. Expected yields with appropriate ranges should be established based on previous laboratory, pilot scale, or manufacturing data. Deviations in yield associated with critical process steps should be investigated to determine their impact or potential impact on the resulting quality of affected batches.

8.15 Any deviation should be documented and explained. Any critical deviation should be investigated.

8.16 The processing status of major units of equipment should be indicated either on the individual units of equipment or by appropriate documentation, computer control systems, or alternative means.

8.17 Materials to be reprocessed or reworked should be appropriately controlled to prevent unauthorized use.

8.2   Time Limits

8.20 If time limits are specified in the master production instruction (see 6.41), these time limits should be met to ensure the quality of intermediates and APIs. Deviations should be documented and evaluated. Time limits may be inappropriate when processing to a target value (e.g., pH adjustment, hydrogenation, drying to predetermined specification) because completion of reactions or processing steps are determined by in-process sampling and testing.

8.21 Intermediates held for further processing should be stored under appropriate conditions to ensure their suitability for use.

8.3   In-process Sampling and Controls

8.30 Written procedures should be established to monitor the progress and control the performance of processing steps that cause variability in the quality characteristics of intermediates and APIs. In-process controls and their acceptance criteria should be defined based on the information gained during the development stage or historical data.

8.31 The acceptance criteria and type and extent of testing can depend on the nature of the intermediate or API being manufactured, the reaction or process step being conducted, and the degree to which the process introduces variability in the product's quality. Less stringent in-process controls may be appropriate in early processing steps, whereas tighter controls may be appropriate for later processing steps (e.g., isolation and purification steps).

8.32 Critical in-process controls (and critical process monitoring), including the control points and methods, should be stated in writing and approved by the quality unit(s).

8.33 In-process controls can be performed by qualified production department personnel and the process adjusted without prior quality unit(s) approval if the adjustments are made within pre-established limits approved by the quality unit(s). All tests and results should be fully documented as part of the batch record.

8.34 Written procedures should describe the sampling methods for in-process materials, intermediates, and APIs. Sampling plans and procedures should be based on scientifically sound sampling practices.

8.35 In-process sampling should be conducted using procedures designed to prevent contamination of the sampled material and other intermediates or APIs.
Procedures should be established to ensure the integrity of samples after collection.

8.36 Out-of-specification (OOS) investigations are not normally needed for in-process tests that are performed for the purpose of monitoring and/or adjusting the process.

8.4 Blending Batches of Intermediates or APIs

8.40 For the purpose of this document, blending is defined as the process of combining materials within the same specification to produce a homogeneous intermediate or API. In-process mixing of fractions from single batches (e.g., collecting several centrifuge loads from a single crystallization batch) or combining fractions from several batches for further processing is considered to be part of the production process and is not considered to be blending.

8.41 Out-Of-Specification batches should not be blended with other batches for the purpose of meeting specifications. Each batch incorporated into the blend should have been manufactured using an established process and should have been individually tested and found to meet appropriate specifications prior to blending.

8.42 Acceptable blending operations include but are not limited to:
- Blending of small batches to increase batch size.
- Blending of tailings (i.e., relatively small quantities of

isolated material) from batches of the same intermediate or API to form a single batch.

8.43 Blending processes should be adequately controlled and documented and the blended batch should be tested for conformance to established specifications where appropriate.

8.44 The batch record of the blending process should allow traceability back to the individual batches that make up the blend.

8.45 Where physical attributes of the API are critical (e.g., APIs intended for use in solid oral dosage forms or suspensions), blending operations should be validated to show homogeneity of the combined batch. Validation should include testing of critical attributes (e.g., particle size distribution, bulk density, and tap density) that may be affected by the blending process.

8.46 If the blending could adversely affect stability, stability testing of the final blended batches should be performed.

8.47 The expiry or retest date of the blended batch should be based on the manufacturing date of the oldest tailings or batch in the blend.

8.5 Contamination Control

8.50 Residual materials can be carried over into successive batches of the same intermediate or API if there is adequate control. Examples include residue adhering to the wall of a micronizer, residual layer of damp crystals remaining in a centrifuge bowl after discharge, and incomplete discharge of fluids or crystals from a processing vessel upon transfer of the material to the next step in the process. Such carryover should not result in the carryover of degradants or microbial contamination that may adversely alter the established API impurity profile.

8.51 Production operations should be conducted in a manner that will prevent contamination of intermediates or APIs by other materials.

8.52 Precautions to avoid contamination should be taken when APIs are handled after purification.

9. PACKAGING AND IDENTIFICATION LABELLING OF APIs AND INTERMEDIATES

9.1 General

9.10 There should be written procedures describing the receipt, identification, quarantine, sampling, examination and/or testing and release, and handling of packaging and labelling materials.

9.11 Packaging and labelling materials should conform to established specifications. Those that do not comply with such specifications should be rejected to prevent their use in operations for which they are unsuitable.

9.12 Records should be maintained for each shipment of labels and packaging materials showing receipt, examination, or testing, and whether accepted or rejected.

9.2   Packaging Materials

9.20 Containers should provide adequate protection against deterioration or contamination of the intermediate or API that may occur during transportation and recommended storage.

9.21 Containers should be clean and, where indicated by the nature of the intermediate or API, sanitized to ensure that they are suitable for their intended use. These containers should not be reactive, additive, or absorptive so as to alter the quality of the intermediate or API beyond the specified limits.

9.22 If containers are re-used, they should be cleaned in accordance with documented procedures and all previous labels should be removed or defaced.

9.3   Label Issuance and Control

9.30 Access to the label storage areas should be limited to authorised personnel.

9.31 Procedures should be used to reconcile the quantities of labels issued, used, and returned and to evaluate discrepancies found between the number of containers labelled and the number of labels issued. Such discrepancies should be investigated, and the investigation should be approved by the quality unit(s).

9.32 All excess labels bearing batch numbers or other batch-related printing should be destroyed. Returned labels should be maintained and stored in a manner that prevents mix-ups and provides proper identification.

9.33 Obsolete and out-dated labels should be destroyed.

9.34 Printing devices used to print labels for packaging operations should be controlled to ensure that all imprinting conforms to the print specified in the batch production record.

9.35 Printed labels issued for a batch should be carefully examined for proper identity and conformity to specifications in the master production record. The results of this examination should be documented.

9.36 A printed label representative of those used should be included in the batch production record.

9.4   Packaging and Labelling Operations

9.40 There should be documented procedures designed to ensure that correct packaging materials and labels are used.

9.41 Labelling operations should be designed to prevent mix-ups. There should be physical or spatial separation from operations involving other intermediates or APIs.

9.42 Labels used on containers of intermediates or APIs should indicate the name or identifying code, the batch number of the product, and storage conditions, when such information is critical to assure the quality of intermediate or API.

9.43 If the intermediate or API is intended to be transferred outside the control of the manufacturer's material management system, the name and address of the manufacturer, quantity of contents, and special transport conditions and any special legal requirements should also be included on the label. For intermediates or APIs with an expiry date, the expiry date should be indicated on the label and Certificate of Analysis. For intermediates or APIs with a retest date, the retest date should be indicated on the label and/or Certificate of Analysis.

9.44 Packaging and labelling facilities should be inspected immediately before use to ensure that all materials not needed for the next packaging operation have been removed. This examination should be documented in the batch production records, the facility log, or other documentation system.

9.45 Packaged and labelled intermediates or APIs should be examined to ensure that containers and packages in the batch have the correct label. This examination should be part of the packaging operation. Results of these examinations should be recorded in the batch production or control records.

9.46 Intermediate or API containers that are transported outside of the manufacturer's control should be sealed in a manner such that, if the seal is breached or missing, the recipient will be alerted to the possibility that the contents may have been altered.

10. STORAGE AND DISTRIBUTION

10.1 Warehousing Procedures

10.10 Facilities should be available for the storage of all materials under appropriate conditions (e.g. controlled temperature and humidity when necessary). Records should be maintained of these conditions if they are critical for the maintenance of material characteristics.

10.11 Unless there is an alternative system to prevent the unintentional or unauthorised use of quarantined, rejected, returned, or recalled materials, separate storage areas should be assigned for their temporary storage until the decision as to their future use has been taken.

10.2 Distribution Procedures

10.20 APIs and intermediates should only be released for distribution to third parties after they have been released by the quality unit(s). APIs and intermediates can be transferred under quarantine to another unit under the company's control when authorized by the quality unit(s) and if appropriate controls and documentation are in place.

10.21 APIs and intermediates should be transported in a manner that does not adversely affect their quality.

10.22 Special transport or storage conditions for an API or intermediate should be stated on the label.

10.23 The manufacturer should ensure that the contract acceptor (contractor) for transportation of the API or intermediate knows and follows the appropriate transport and storage conditions.

10.24 A system should be in place by which the distribution of each batch of intermediate and/or API can be readily determined to permit its recall.

11. LABORATORY CONTROLS

11.1 General Controls

11.10 The independent quality unit(s) should have at its disposal adequate laboratory facilities.

11.11 There should be documented procedures describing sampling, testing, approval or rejection of materials, and recording and storage of laboratory data. Laboratory records should be maintained in accordance with Section 6.6.

11.12 All specifications, sampling plans, and test procedures should be scientifically sound and appropriate to ensure that raw materials, intermediates, APIs, and labels and packaging materials conform to established standards of quality and/or purity. Specifications and test procedures should be consistent with those included in the registration/filing. There can be specifications in addition to those in the registration/filing. Specifications, sampling plans, and test procedures, including changes to them, should be drafted by the appropriate organizational unit and reviewed and approved by the quality unit(s).

11.13 Appropriate specifications should be established for APIs in accordance with accepted standards and consistent with the manufacturing process. The specifications should include a control of the impurities (e.g. organic impurities, inorganic impurities, and residual solvents). If the API has a specification for microbiological purity, appropriate action limits for total microbial counts and objectionable organisms should be established and met. If the API has a specification for endotoxins, appropriate action limits should be established and met.

11.14 Laboratory controls should be followed and documented at the time of performance. Any departures from the above described procedures should be documented and explained.

11.15 Any out-of-specification result obtained should be investigated and documented according to a procedure. This procedure should require analysis of the data, assessment of whether a significant problem exists, allocation of the tasks for corrective actions, and conclusions. Any resampling and/or retesting after OOS results should be performed according to a documented procedure.

11.16 Reagents and standard solutions should be prepared and labelled following written procedures. "Use by" dates should be applied as appropriate for analytical reagents or standard solutions.

11.17 Primary reference standards should be obtained as appropriate for the manufacture of APIs. The source of each primary reference standard should be documented. Records should be maintained of each primary reference standard's storage and use in accordance with the supplier's recommendations. Primary reference standards obtained from an officially recognised source are normally used without testing if stored under conditions consistent with the supplier's recommendations.

11.18 Where a primary reference standard is not available from an officially recognized source, an "in-house primary standard" should be established. Appropriate testing should be performed to establish fully the identity and purity of the primary reference standard. Appropriate documentation of this testing should be maintained.

11.19 Secondary reference standards should be appropriately prepared, identified, tested, approved, and stored. The suitability of each batch of secondary reference standard should be determined prior to first use by comparing against a primary reference standard. Each batch of secondary reference standard should be periodically requalified in accordance with a written protocol.

11.2 Testing of Intermediates and APIs

11.20 For each batch of intermediate and API, appropriate laboratory tests should be conducted to determine conformance to specifications.

11.21 An impurity profile describing the identified and unidentified impurities present in a typical batch produced by a specific controlled production process should normally be established for each API. The impurity profile should include the identity or some qualitative analytical designation (e.g. retention time), the range of each impurity observed, and classification of each identified impurity (e.g. inorganic, organic, solvent). The impurity profile is normally dependent upon the production process and origin of the API. Impurity profiles are normally not necessary for APIs from herbal or animal tissue origin. Biotechnology considerations are covered in ICH Guideline Q6B.

11.22 The impurity profile should be compared at appropriate intervals against the impurity profile in the regulatory submission or compared against historical data in order to detect changes to the API resulting from modifications in raw materials, equipment operating parameters, or the production process.

11.23 Appropriate microbiological tests should be conducted on each batch of intermediate and API where microbial quality is specified.

11.3 Validation of Analytical Procedures - see Section 12.

11.4 Certificates of Analysis

11.40 Authentic Certificates of Analysis should be issued for each batch of intermediate or API on request.

11.41 Information on the name of the intermediate or API including where appropriate its grade, the batch number, and the date of release should be provided on the Certificate of Analysis. For intermediates or APIs with an expiry date, the expiry date should be provided on the label and Certificate of Analysis. For intermediates or APIs with a retest date, the retest date should be indicated on the label and/or Certificate of Analysis.

11.42 The Certificate should list each test performed in accordance with compendial or customer requirements, including the acceptance limits, and the numerical results obtained (if test results are numerical).

11.43 Certificates should be dated and signed by authorised personnel of the quality unit(s) and should show the name, address and telephone number of the original manufacturer. Where the analysis has been carried out by a repacker or reprocessor, the Certificate of Analysis should show the name, address and telephone number of the repacker/reprocessor and a reference to the name of the original manufacturer.

11.44 If new Certificates are issued by or on behalf of repackers/reprocessors, agents or brokers, these Certificates should show the name, address and telephone number of the laboratory that performed the analysis. They should also contain a reference to the name and address of the original manufacturer and to the original batch Certificate, a copy of which should be attached.

11.5 Stability Monitoring of APIs

11.50 A documented, on-going testing program should be designed to monitor the stability characteristics of APIs, and the results should be used to confirm appropriate storage conditions and retest or expiry dates.

11.51 The test procedures used in stability testing should be validated and be stability indicating.

11.52 Stability samples should be stored in containers that

simulate the market container. For example, if the API is marketed in bags within fiber drums, stability samples can be packaged in bags of the same material and in smaller-scale drums of similar or identical material composition to the market drums.

11.53 Normally the first three commercial production batches should be placed on the stability monitoring program to confirm the retest or expiry date. However, where data from previous studies show that the API is expected to remain stable for at least two years, fewer than three batches can be used.

11.54 Thereafter, at least one batch per year of API manufactured (unless none is produced that year) should be added to the stability monitoring program and tested at least annually to confirm the stability.

11.55 For APIs with short shelf-lives, testing should be done more frequently. For example, for those biotechnological/biologic and other APIs with shelf-lives of one year or less, stability samples should be obtained and should be tested monthly for the first three months, and at three month intervals after that. When data exist that confirm that the stability of the API is not compromised, elimination of specific test intervals (e.g. 9 month testing) can be considered.

11.56 Where appropriate, the stability storage conditions should be consistent with the ICH guidelines on stability.

11.6 Expiry and Retest Dating

11.60 When an intermediate is intended to be transferred outside the control of the manufacturer's material management system and an expiry or retest date is assigned, supporting stability information should be available (e.g. published data, test results).

11.61 An API expiry or retest date should be based on an evaluation of data derived from stability studies. Common practice is to use a retest date, not an expiration date.

11.62 Preliminary API expiry or retest dates can be based on pilot scale batches if (1) the pilot batches employ a method of manufacture and procedure that simulates the final process to be used on a commercial manufacturing scale; and (2) the quality of the API represents the material to be made on a commercial scale.

11.63 A representative sample should be taken for the purpose of performing a retest.

11.7 Reserve/Retention Samples

11.70 The packaging and holding of reserve samples is for the purpose of potential future evaluation of the quality of batches of API and not for future stability testing purposes.

11.71 Appropriately identified reserve samples of each API batch should be retained for one year after the expiry date of the batch assigned by the manufacturer, or for three years after distribution of the batch, whichever is the longer. For APIs with retest dates, similar reserve samples should be retained for three years after the batch is completely distributed by the manufacturer.

11.72 The reserve sample should be stored in the same packaging system in which the API is stored or in one that is equivalent to or more protective than the marketed packaging system. Sufficient quantities should be retained to conduct at least two full compendial analyses or, when there is no pharmacopoeial monograph, two full specification analyses.

12. VALIDATION

12.1 Validation Policy

12.10 The company's overall policy, intentions, and approach to validation, including the validation of production processes, cleaning procedures, analytical methods, in-process control test procedures, computerized systems, and persons responsible for design, review, approval and documentation of each validation phase, should be documented.

12.11 The critical parameters/attributes should normally be identified during the development stage or from historical data, and the ranges necessary for the reproducible operation should be defined. This should include:
- Defining the API in terms of its critical product attributes;
- Identifying process parameters that could affect the critical quality attributes of the API;
- Determining the range for each critical process parameter expected to be used during routine manufacturing and process control.

12.12 Validation should extend to those operations determined to be critical to the quality and purity of the API.

12.2 Validation Documentation

12.20 A written validation protocol should be established that specifies how validation of a particular process will be conducted. The protocol should be reviewed and approved by the quality unit(s) and other designated units.

12.21 The validation protocol should specify critical process steps and acceptance criteria as well as the type of validation to be conducted (e.g. retrospective, prospective, concurrent) and the number of process runs.

12.22 A validation report that cross-references the validation protocol should be prepared, summarising the results obtained, commenting on any deviations observed, and drawing the appropriate conclusions, including recommending changes to correct deficiencies.

12.23 Any variations from the validation protocol should be documented with appropriate justification.

12.3 Qualification

12.30 Before starting process validation activities, appropriate qualification of critical equipment and ancillary systems should be completed. Qualification is usually carried out by conducting the following activities, individually or combined:

- Design Qualification (DQ): documented verification that the proposed design of the facilities, equipment, or systems is suitable for the intended purpose.
- Installation Qualification (IQ): documented verification that the equipment or systems, as installed or modified, comply with the approved design, the manufacturer's recommendations and/or user requirements.
- Operational Qualification (OQ): documented verification that the equipment or systems, as installed or modified, perform as intended throughout the anticipated operating ranges.
- Performance Qualification (PQ): documented verification that the equipment and ancillary systems, as connected together, can perform effectively and reproducibly based on the approved process method and specifications.

12.4 Approaches to Process Validation

12.40 Process Validation (PV) is the documented evidence that the process, operated within established parameters, can perform effectively and reproducibly to produce an intermediate or API meeting its predetermined specifications and quality attributes.

12.41 There are three approaches to validation. Prospective validation is the preferred approach, but there are exceptions where the other approaches can be used. These approaches and their applicability are listed below. 12.42 Prospective validation should normally be performed for all API processes as defined in 12.12. Prospective validation performed on an API process should be completed before the commercial distribution of the final drug product manufactured from that API.

12.43 Concurrent validation can be conducted when data from replicate production runs are unavailable because only a limited number of API batches have been produced, API batches are produced infrequently, or API batches are produced by a validated process that has been modified. Prior to the completion of concurrent validation, batches can be released and used in final drug product for commercial distribution based on thorough monitoring and testing of the API batches.

12.44 An exception can be made for retrospective validation for well established processes that have been used without significant changes to API quality due to changes in raw materials, equipment, systems, facilities, or the production process. This validation approach may be used where:

(1) Critical quality attributes and critical process parameters have been identified;

(2) Appropriate in-process acceptance criteria and controls have been established;

(3) There have not been significant process/product failures attributable to causes other than operator error or equipment failures unrelated to equipment suitability; and

(4) Impurity profiles have been established for the existing API.

12.45 Batches selected for retrospective validation should be representative of all batches made during the review period, including any batches that failed to meet specifications, and should be sufficient in number to demonstrate process consistency. Retained samples can be tested to obtain data to retrospectively validate the process.

12.5 Process Validation Program

12.50 The number of process runs for validation should depend on the complexity of the process or the magnitude of the process change being considered. For prospective and concurrent validation, three consecutive successful production batches should be used as a guide, but there may be situations where additional process runs are warranted to prove consistency of the process (e.g., complex API processes or API processes with prolonged completion times). For retrospective validation, generally data from ten to thirty consecutive batches should be examined to assess process consistency, but fewer batches can be examined if justified.

12.51 Critical process parameters should be controlled and monitored during process validation studies. Process parameters unrelated to quality, such as variables controlled to minimize energy consumption or equipment use, need not be included in the process validation.

12.52 Process validation should confirm that the impurity profile for each API is within the limits specified. The impurity profile should be comparable to or better than historical data and, where applicable, the profile determined during process development or for batches used for pivotal clinical and toxicological studies.

12.6 Periodic Review of Validated Systems

12.60 Systems and processes should be periodically evaluated to verify that they are still operating in a valid manner. Where no significant changes have been made to the system or process, and a quality review confirms that the system or process is consistently producing material meeting its specifications, there is normally no need for revalidation.

12.7 Cleaning Validation

12.70 Cleaning procedures should normally be validated. In general, cleaning validation should be directed to situations or process steps where contamination or carryover of materials poses the greatest risk to API quality. For example, in early production it may be unnecessary to validate equipment cleaning procedures where residues are removed by subsequent purification steps.

12.71 Validation of cleaning procedures should reflect actual equipment usage patterns. If various APIs or intermediates are manufactured in the same equipment and the equipment is cleaned by the same process, a representative intermediate or API can be selected for cleaning validation. This selection should be based on the solubility and difficulty of cleaning and the calculation of residue limits based on potency, toxicity, and stability.

12.72 The cleaning validation protocol should describe the equipment to be cleaned, procedures, materials, acceptable cleaning levels, parameters to be monitored and controlled, and analytical methods. The protocol should also indicate the type of samples to be obtained and how they are collected and labelled.

12.73 Sampling should include swabbing, rinsing, or alternative methods (e.g., direct extraction), as appropriate, to detect both insoluble and soluble residues. The sampling methods used should be capable of quantitatively measuring levels of residues remaining on the equipment surfaces after cleaning. Swab sampling may be impractical when product contact surfaces are not easily accessible due to equipment design and/or process limitations (e.g., inner surfaces of hoses, transfer pipes, reactor tanks with small ports or handling toxic materials, and small intricate equipment such as micronizers and microfluidizers).

12.74 Validated analytical methods having sensitivity to detect residues or contaminants should be used. The detection limit for each analytical method should be sufficiently sensitive to detect the established acceptable level of the residue or contaminant. The method's attainable recovery level should be established. Residue limits should be practical, achievable, verifiable and based on the most deleterious residue. Limits can be established based on the minimum known pharmacological, toxicological, or physiological activity of the API or its most deleterious component.

12.75 Equipment cleaning/sanitization studies should address microbiological and endotoxin contamination for those processes where there is a need to reduce total microbiological count or endotoxins in the API, or other processes where such contamination could be of concern (e.g., non-sterile APIs used to manufacture sterile products).

12.76 Cleaning procedures should be monitored at appropriate intervals after validation to ensure that these procedures are effective when used during routine production. Equipment cleanliness can be monitored by analytical testing and visual examination, where feasible. Visual inspection can allow detection of gross contamination concentrated in small areas that could otherwise go undetected by sampling and/or analysis.

12.8 Validation of Analytical Methods

12.80 Analytical methods should be validated unless the method employed is included in the relevant pharmacopoeia or other recognised standard reference. The suitability of all testing methods used should nonetheless be verified under actual conditions of use and documented.

12.81 Methods should be validated to include consideration of characteristics included within the ICH guidelines on validation of analytical methods. The degree of analytical validation performed should reflect the purpose of the analysis and the stage of the API production process.

12.82 Appropriate qualification of analytical equipment should be considered before starting validation of analytical methods.

12.83 Complete records should be maintained of any modification of a validated analytical method. Such records should include the reason for the modification and appropriate data to verify that the modification produces results that are as accurate and reliable as the established method.

13. CHANGE CONTROL

13.10 A formal change control system should be established to evaluate all changes that may affect the production and control of the intermediate or API.

13.11 Written procedures should provide for the identification, documentation, appropriate review, and approval of changes in raw materials, specifications, analytical methods, facilities, support systems, equipment (including computer hardware), processing steps, labelling and packaging lmaterials, and computer software.

13.12 Any proposals for GMP relevant changes should be drafted, reviewed, and approved by the appropriate organisational units, and reviewed and approved by the quality unit(s).

13.13 The potential impact of the proposed change on the quality of the intermediate or API should be evaluated. A classification procedure may help in determining the level of testing, validation, and documentation needed to justify changes to a validated process. Changes can be classified (e.g. as minor or major) depending on the nature and extent of the changes, and the effects these changes may impart on the process. Scientific judgement should determine what additional testing and validation studies are appropriate to justify a change in a validated process.

13.14 When implementing approved changes, measures should be taken to ensure that all documents affected by the changes are revised.

13.15 After the change has been implemented, there should be an evaluation of the first batches produced or tested under the change.

13.16 The potential for critical changes to affect established retest or expiry dates should be evaluated. If necessary, samples of the intermediate or API produced by the modified process can be placed on an accelerated stability program and/or can be added to the stability monitoring program.

13.17 Current dosage form manufacturers should be notified of changes from established production and process control procedures that can impact the quality of the API.

14. REJECTION AND RE-USE OF MATERIALS

14.1 Rejection

14.10 Intermediates and APIs failing to meet established specifications should be identified as such and quarantined. These intermediates or APIs can be reprocessed or reworked as described below. The final disposition of rejected materials should be recorded.

14.2 Reprocessing

14.20 Introducing an intermediate or API, including one that does not conform to standards or specifications, back into the process and reprocessing by repeating a crystallization step or other appropriate chemical or physical manipulation steps (e.g., distillation, filtration, chromatography, milling) that are part of the established manufacturing process is generally considered acceptable. However, if such reprocessing is used for a majority of batches, such reprocessing should be included as part of the standard manufacturing process.

14.21 Continuation of a process step after an in-process control test has shown that the step is incomplete is considered to be part of the normal process. This is not considered to be reprocessing.

14.22 Introducing unreacted material back into a process and repeating a chemical reaction is considered to be reprocessing unless it is part of the established process. Such reprocessing should be preceded by careful evaluation to ensure that the quality of the intermediate or API is not adversely impacted due to the potential formation of by-products and over-reacted materials.

14.3 Reworking

14.30 Before a decision is taken to rework batches that do not conform to established standards or specifications, an investigation into the reason for non-conformance should be performed.

14.31 Batches that have been reworked should be subjected to appropriate evaluation, testing, stability testing if warranted, and documentation to show that the reworked product is of equivalent quality to that produced by the original process. Concurrent validation is often the appropriate validation approach for rework procedures. This allows a protocol to define the rework procedure, how it will be carried out, and the expected results. If there is only one batch to be reworked, then a report can be written and the batch released once it is found to be acceptable.

14.32 Procedures should provide for comparing the impurity profile of each reworked batch against batches manufactured by the established process. Where routine analytical methods are inadequate to characterize the reworked batch, additional methods should be used.

14.4 Recovery of Materials and Solvents

14.40 Recovery (e.g. from mother liquor or filtrates) of reactants, intermediates, or the API is considered acceptable, provided that approved procedures exist for the recovery and the recovered materials meet specifications suitable for their intended use.

14.41 Solvents can be recovered and reused in the same processes or in different processes, provided that the recovery procedures are controlled and monitored to ensure that solvents meet appropriate standards before reuse or co-mingling with other approved materials.

14.42 Fresh and recovered solvents and reagents can be combined if adequate testing has shown their suitability for all manufacturing processes in which they may be used.

14.43 The use of recovered solvents, mother liquors, and other recovered materials should be adequately documented.

14.5 Returns

14.50 Returned intermediates or APIs should be identified as such and quarantined.

14.51 If the conditions under which returned intermediates or APIs have been stored or shipped before or during their return or the condition of their containers casts doubt on their quality, the returned intermediates or APIs should be reprocessed, reworked, or destroyed, as appropriate.

14.52 Records of returned intermediates or APIs should be maintained. For each return, documentation should include:
- Name and address of the consignee
- Intermediate or API, batch number, and quantity returned
- Reason for return
- Use or disposal of the returned intermediate or API

15. COMPLAINTS AND RECALLS

15.10 All quality related complaints, whether received orally or in writing, should be recorded and investigated according to a written procedure.

15.11 Complaint records should include:
- Name and address of complainant;
- Name (and, where appropriate, title) and phone number of person submitting the complaint;
- Complaint nature (including name and batch number of the API);
- Date complaint is received;
- Action initially taken (including dates and identity of person taking the action);
- Any follow-up action taken;
- Response provided to the originator of complaint (including date response sent); and
- Final decision on intermediate or API batch or lot.

15.12 Records of complaints should be retained in order to evaluate trends, product-related frequencies, and severity with a view to taking additional, and if appropriate, immediate corrective action.

15.13 There should be a written procedure that defines the circumstances under which a recall of an intermediate or API should be considered.

15.14 The recall procedure should designate who should be involved in evaluating the information, how a recall should be initiated, who should be informed about the recall, and how the recalled material should be treated.

15.15 In the event of a serious or potentially life-threatening situation, local, national, and/or international authorities should be informed and their advice sought.

16. CONTRACT MANUFACTURERS (INCLUDING LABORATORIES)

16.10 All contract manufacturers (including laboratories) should comply with the GMP defined in this Guide. Special consideration should be given to the prevention of cross-contamination and to maintaining traceability.

16.11 Contract manufacturers (including laboratories) should be evaluated by the contract giver to ensure GMP compliance of the specific operations occurring at the contract sites.

16.12 There should be a written and approved contract or formal agreement between the contract giver and the contract acceptor that defines in detail the GMP responsibilities, including the quality measures, of each party.

16.13 The contract should permit the contract giver to audit the contract acceptor's facilities for compliance with GMP.

16.14 Where subcontracting is allowed, the contract acceptor should not pass to a third party any of the work entrusted to him under the contract without the contract giver's prior evaluation and approval of the arrangements.

16.15 Manufacturing and laboratory records should be kept at the site where the activity occurs and be readily available.

16.16 Changes in the process, equipment, test methods, specifications, or other contractual requirements should not be made unless the contract giver is informed and approves the changes.

17. AGENTS, BROKERS, TRADERS, DISTRIBUTORS, REPACKERS, AND RELABELLERS

17.1 Applicability

17.10 This section applies to any party other than the original manufacturer who may trade and/or take possession, repack, relabel, manipulate, distribute or store an API or intermediate.

17.11 All agents, brokers, traders, distributors, repackers, and relabellers should comply with GMP as defined in this Guide.

17.2 Traceability of Distributed APIs and Intermediates

17.20 Agents, brokers, traders, distributors, repackers, or relabellers should maintain complete traceability of APIs and intermediates that they distribute. Documents that should be retained and available include:
- Identity of original manufacturer
- Address of original manufacturer

- Purchase orders
- Bills of lading (transportation documentation)
- Receipt documents
- Name or designation of API or intermediate
- Manufacturer's batch number
- Transportation and distribution records
- All authentic Certificates of Analysis, including those of the original manufacturer
- Retest or expiry date

17.3 Quality Management

17.30 Agents, brokers, traders, distributors, repackers, or relabellers should establish, document and implement an effective system of managing quality, as specified in Section 2.

17.4 Repackaging, Relabelling and Holding of APIs and Intermediates

17.40 Repackaging, relabelling and holding of APIs and intermediates should be performed under appropriate GMP controls, as stipulated in this Guide, to avoid mix-ups and loss of API or intermediate identity or purity.

17.41 Repackaging should be conducted under appropriate environmental conditions to avoid contamination and cross-contamination.

17.5 Stability

17.50 Stability studies to justify assigned expiration or retest dates should be conducted if the API or intermediate is repackaged in a different type of container than that used by the API or intermediate manufacturer.

17.6 Transfer of Information

17.60 Agents, brokers, distributors, repackers, or relabellers should transfer all quality or regulatory information received from an API or intermediate manufacturer to the customer, and from the customer to the API or intermediate manufacturer.

17.61 The agent, broker, trader, distributor, repacker, or relabeller who supplies the API or intermediate to the customer should provide the name of the original API or intermediate manufacturer and the batch number(s) supplied.

17.62 The agent should also provide the identity of the original API or intermediate manufacturer to regulatory authorities upon request. The original manufacturer can respond to the regulatory authority directly or through its authorized agents, depending on the legal relationship between the authorized agents and the original API or intermediate manufacturer. (In this context "authorized" refers to authorized by the manufacturer.)

17.63 The specific guidance for Certificates of Analysis included in Section 11.4 should be met.

17.7 Handling of Complaints and Recalls

17.70 Agents, brokers, traders, distributors, repackers, or relabellers should maintain records of complaints and recalls, as specified in Section 15, for all complaints and recalls that come to their attention.

17.71 If the situation warrants, the agents, brokers, traders, distributors, repackers, or relabellers should review the complaint with the original API or intermediate manufacturer in order to determine whether any further action, either with other customers who may have received this API or intermediate or with the regulatory authority, or both, should be initiated. The investigation into the cause for the complaint or recall should be conducted and documented by the appropriate party.

17.72 Where a complaint is referred to the original API or intermediate manufacturer, the record maintained by the agents, brokers, traders, distributors, repackers, or relabellers should include any response received from the original API or intermediate manufacturer (including date and information provided).

17.8 Handling of Returns

17.80 Returns should be handled as specified in Section 14.52. The agents, brokers, traders, distributors, repackers, or relabellers should maintain documentation of returned APIs and intermediates.

18. SPECIFIC GUIDANCE FOR APIs MANUFACTURED BY CELL CULTURE/FERMENTATION

18.1 General

18.10 Section 18 is intended to address specific controls for APIs or intermediates manufactured by cell culture or fermentation using natural or rocombinant organisms and that have not been covered adequately in the previous sections. It is not intended to be a stand-alone Section. In general, the GMP principles in the other sections of this document apply. Note that the principles of fermentation for "classical" processes for production of small molecules and for processes using recombinant and non-recombinant organisms for production of proteins and/or polypeptides are the same, although the degree of control will differ. Where practical, this section will address these differences. In general, the degree of control for biotechnological processes used to produce proteins and polypeptides is greater than that for classical fermentation processes.

18.11 The term "biotechnological process" (biotech) refers to the use of cells or organisms that have been generated or modified by recombinant DNA, hybridoma or other technology to produce APIs. The APIs produced by biotechnological processes normally consist of high molecular weight substances, such as proteins and polypeptides, for which specific guidance is given in this Section. Certain APIs of low molecular weight, such as antibiotics, amino acids, vitamins, and carbohydrates, can also be produced by recombinant DNA technology. The level of control for these types of APIs is similar to that employed for classical fermentation.

18.12 The term "classical fermentation" refers to processes that use microorganisms existing in nature and/or modified by conventional methods (e.g. irradiation or chemical mutagenesis) to produce APIs. APIs produced by "classical fermentation" are normally low molecular weight products such as antibiotics, amino acids, vitamins, and carbohydrates.

18.13 Production of APIs or intermediates from cell culture or fermentation involves biological processes such as cultivation of cells or extraction and purification of material from living organisms. Note that there may be additional process steps, such as physicochemical modification, that are part of the manufacturing process. The raw materials used (media, buffer components) may provide the potential for growth of microbiological contaminants. Depending on the source, method of preparation, and the intended use of the API or intermediate, control of bioburden, viral contamination, and/or endotoxins during manufacturing and monitoring of the process at appropriate stages may be necessary.

18.14 Appropriate controls should be established at all stages of manufacturing to assure intermediate and/or API quality. While this Guide starts at the cell culture/fermentation step, prior steps (e.g. cell banking) should be performed under appropriate process controls. This Guide covers cell culture/fermentation from the point at which a vial of the cell bank is retrieved for use in manufacturing.

18.15 Appropriate equipment and environmental controls should be used to minimize the risk of contamination. The acceptance criteria for quality of the environment and the frequency of monitoring should depend on the step in production and the production conditions (open, closed, or contained systems).

18.16 In general, process controls should take into account:
- Maintenance of the Working Cell Bank (where appropriate);
- Proper inoculation and expansion of the culture;
- Control of the critical operating parameters during fermentation/cell culture;
- Monitoring of the process for cell growth, viability (for most cell culture processes) and productivity where appropriate;
- Harvest and purification procedures that remove cells, cellular debris and media components while protecting the intermediate or API from contamination (particularly of a microbiological nature) and from loss of quality;
- Monitoring of bioburden and, where needed, endotoxin levels at appropriate stages of production; and
- Viral safety concerns as described in ICH Guideline Q5A Quality of Biotechnological Products: Viral Safety Evaluation of Biotechnology Products Derived from Cell Lines of Human or Animal Origin.

18.17 Where appropriate, the removal of media components, host cell proteins, other process-related impurities, product-related impurities and contaminants should be demonstrated.

18.2 Cell Bank Maintenance and Record Keeping

18.20 Access to cell banks should be limited to authorized personnel.

18.21 Cell banks should be maintained under storage conditions designed to maintain viability and prevent contamination.

18.22 Records of the use of the vials from the cell banks and storage conditions should be maintained.

18.23 Where appropriate, cell banks should be periodically monitored to determine suitability for use.

18.24 See ICH Guideline Q5D Quality of Biotechnological Products: Derivation and Characterization of Cell Substrates Used for Production of Biotechnological/ Biological Products for a more complete discussion of cell banking.

18.3 Cell Culture/Fermentation

18.30 Where aseptic addition of cell substrates, media, buffers, and gases is needed, closed or contained systems should be used where possible. If the inoculation of the initial vessel or subsequent transfers or additions (media, buffers) are performed in open vessels, there should be controls and procedures in place to minimize the risk of contamination.

18.31 Where the quality of the API can be affected by microbial contamination, manipulations using open vessels should be performed in a biosafety cabinet or similarly controlled environment.

18.32 Personnel should be appropriately gowned and take special precautions handling the cultures.

18.33 Critical operating parameters (for example temperature, pH, agitation rates, addition of gases, pressure) should be monitored to ensure consistency with the established process. Cell growth, viability (for most cell culture processes), and, where appropriate, productivity should also be monitored. Critical parameters will vary from one process to another, and for classical fermentation, certain parameters (cell viability, for example) may not need to be monitored.

18.34 Cell culture equipment should be cleaned and sterilized after use. As appropriate, fermentation equipment should be cleaned, and sanitized or sterilized.

18.35 Culture media should be sterilized before use when appropriate to protect the quality of the API.

18.36 There should be appropriate procedures in place to detect contamination and determine the course of action to be taken. This should include procedures to determine the impact of the contamination on the product and those to decontaminate the equipment and return it to a condition to be used insubsequent batches. Foreign organisms observed during fermentation processes should be identified as appropriate and the effect of their presence on product quality should be assessed, if necessary. The results of such assessments should be taken into consideration in the disposition of the material produced.

18.37 Records of contamination events should be maintained.

18.38 Shared (multi-product) equipment may warrant additional testing after cleaning between product campaigns, as appropriate, to minimize the risk of cross-contamination.

18.4 Harvesting, Isolation and Purification

18.40 Harvesting steps, either to remove cells or cellular components or to collect cellular components after disruption, should be performed in equipment and areas designed to minimize the risk of contamination.

18.41 Harvest and purification procedures that remove or inactivate the producing organism, cellular debris and media components (while minimizing degradation, contamination, and loss of quality) should be adequate to ensure that the intermediate or API is recovered with consistent quality.

18.42 All equipment should be properly cleaned and, as appropriate, sanitized after use.
Multiple successive batching without cleaning can be used if intermediate or API quality is not compromised.

18.43 If open systems are used, purification should be performed under environmental conditions appropriate for the preservation of product quality.

18.44 Additional controls, such as the use of dedicated chromatography resins or additional testing, may be appropriate if equipment is to be used for multiple products.

18.5 Viral Removal/Inactivation steps

18.50 See the ICH Guideline Q5A Quality of Biotechnological Products: Viral Safety Evaluation of Biotechnology Products Derived from Cell Lines of Human or Animal Origin for more specific information.

18.51 Viral removal and viral inactivation steps are critical processing steps for some processes and should be performed within their validated parameters.

18.52 Appropriate precautions should be taken to prevent potential viral contamination from pre-viral to post-viral removal/inactivation steps. Therefore, open processing should be performed in areas that are separate from other processing activities and have separate air handling units.

18.53 The same equipment is not normally used for different purification steps. However, if the same equipment is to be used, the equipment should be appropriately cleaned and sanitized before reuse. Appropriate precautions should be taken to prevent potential virus carry-over (e.g. through equipment or environment) from previous steps.

19. APIs FOR USE IN CLINICAL TRIALS

19.1 General

19.10 Not all the controls in the previous sections of this Guide are appropriate for the manufacture of a new API for investigational use during its development. Section 19 provides specific guidance unique to these circumstances.

19.11 The controls used in the manufacture of APIs for use in clinical trials should be consistent with the stage of development of the drug product incorporating the API. Process and test procedures should be flexible to provide for changes as knowledge of the process increases and clinical testing of a drug product progresses from pre-clinical stages through clinical stages. Once drug development reaches the stage where the API is produced for use in drug products intended for clinical trials, manufacturers should ensure that APIs are manufactured in suitable facilities using appropriate production and control procedures to ensure the quality of the API.

19.2 Quality

19.20 Appropriate GMP concepts should be applied in the production of APIs for use in clinical trials with a suitable mechanism of approval of each batch.

19.21 A quality unit(s) independent from production should be established for the approval or rejection of each batch of API for use in clinical trials.

19.22 Some of the testing functions commonly performed by the quality unit(s) can be performed within other organizational units.

19.23 Quality measures should include a system for testing of raw materials, packaging materials, intermediates, and APIs.

19.24 Process and quality problems should be evaluated.

19.25 Labelling for APIs intended for use in clinical trials should be appropriately controlled and should identify the material as being for investigational use.

19.3 Equipment and Facilities

19.30 During all phases of clinical development, including the use of small-scale facilities or laboratories to manufacture batches of APIs for use in clinical trials, procedures should be in place to ensure that equipment is calibrated, clean and suitable for its intended use.

19.31 Procedures for the use of facilities should ensure that materials are handled in a manner that minimizes the risk of contamination and cross-contamination.

19.4 Control of Raw Materials

19.40 Raw materials used in production of APIs for use in clinical trials should be evaluated by testing, or received with a supplier's analysis and subjected to identity testing. When a material is considered hazardous, a supplier's analysis should suffice.

19.41 In some instances, the suitability of a raw material can be determined before use based on acceptability in small-scale reactions (i.e., use testing) rather than on analytical testing alone.

19.5 Production

19.50 The production of APIs for use in clinical trials should be documented in laboratory notebooks, batch records, or by other appropriate means. These documents should include information on the use of production materials, equipment, processing, and scientific observations.

19.51 Expected yields can be more variable and less defined than the expected yields used in commercial processes. Investigations into yield variations are not expected.

19.6 Validation

19.60 Process validation for the production of APIs for use in clinical trials is normally inappropriate, where a single API batch is produced or where process changes during API development make batch replication difficult or inexact. The combination of controls, calibration, and, where appropriate, equipment qualification assures API quality during this development phase.

19.61 Process validation should be conducted in accordance with Section 12 when batches are produced for commercial use, even when such batches are produced on a pilot or small scale.

19.7 Changes

19.70 Changes are expected during development, as knowledge is gained and the production is scaled up. Every change in the production, specifications, or test procedures should be adequately recorded.

19.8 Laboratory Controls

19.80 While analytical methods performed to evaluate a batch of API for clinical trials may not yet be validated, they should be scientifically sound.

19.81 A system for retaining reserve samples of all batches should be in place. This system should ensure that a sufficient quantity of each reserve sample is retained for an appropriate length of time after approval, termination, or discontinuation of an application.

19.82 Expiry and retest dating as defined in Section 11.6 applies to existing APIs used in clinical trials. For new APIs, Section 11.6 does not normally apply in early stages of clinical trials.

19.9 Documentation

19.90 A system should be in place to ensure that information gained during the development and the manufacture of APIs for use in clinical trials is documented and available.

19.91 The development and implementation of the analytical methods used to support the release of a batch of API for use in clinical trials should be appropriately documented.

19.92 A system for retaining production and control records and documents should be used. This system should ensure that records and documents are retained for an appropriate length of time after the approval, termination, or discontinuation of an application.

20. GLOSSARY

Acceptance Criteria
Numerical limits, ranges, or other suitable measures for acceptance of test results.

Active Pharmaceutical Ingredient (API) (or Drug Substance)
Any substance or mixture of substances intended to be used in the manufacture of a drug (medicinal) product and that, when used in the production of a drug, becomes an active ingredient of the drug product. Such substances are intended to furnish pharmacological activity or other direct effect in the diagnosis, cure, mitigation, treatment, or prevention of disease or to affect the structure and function of the body.

API Starting Material
A raw material, intermediate, or an API that is used in the production of an API and that is incorporated as a significant structural fragment into the structure of the API. An API Starting Material can be an article of commerce, a material purchased from one or more suppliers under contract or commercial agreement, or produced in-house. API Starting Materials are normally of defined chemical properties and structure.

Batch (or Lot)
A specific quantity of material produced in a process or series of processes so that it is expected to be homogeneous within specified limits. In the case of continuous production, a batch may correspond to a defined fraction of the production. The batch size can be defined either by a fixed quantity or by the amount produced in a fixed time interval.

Batch Number (or Lot Number)
A unique combination of numbers, letters, and/or symbols that identifies a batch (or lot) and from which the production and distribution history can be determined.

Bioburden
The level and type (e.g. objectionable or not) of micro-organisms that can be present in raw materials, API starting materials, intermediates or APIs. Bioburden should not be considered contamination unless the levels have been exceeded or defined objectionable organisms have been detected.

Calibration
The demonstration that a particular instrument or device produces results within specified limits by comparison with those produced

by a reference or traceable standard over an appropriate range of measurements.

Computer System
A group of hardware components and associated software, designed and assembled to perform a specific function or group of functions.

Computerized System
A process or operation integrated with a computer system.

Contamination
The undesired introduction of impurities of a chemical or microbiological nature, or of foreign matter, into or onto a raw material, intermediate, or API during production, sampling, packaging or repackaging, storage or transport.

Contract Manufacturer
A manufacturer performing some aspect of manufacturing on behalf of the original manufacturer.

Critical
Describes a process step, process condition, test requirement, or other relevant parameter or item that must be controlled within predetermined criteria to ensure that the API meets its specification.

Cross-Contamination
Contamination of a material or product with another material or product.

Deviation
Departure from an approved instruction or established standard.

Drug (Medicinal) Product
The dosage form in the final immediate packaging intended for marketing. (Reference Q1A)

Drug Substance
See Active Pharmaceutical Ingredient

Expiry Date (or Expiration Date)
The date placed on the container/labels of an API designating the time during which the API is expected to remain within established shelf life specifications if stored under defined conditions, and after which it should not be used.

Impurity
Any component present in the intermediate or API that is not the desired entity.

Impurity Profile
A description of the identified and unidentified impurities present in an API.

In-Process Control (or Process Control)
Checks performed during production in order to monitor and, if appropriate, to adjust the process and/or to ensure that the intermediate or API conforms to its specifications.

Intermediate
A material produced during steps of the processing of an API that undergoes further molecular change or purification before it becomes an API. Intermediates may or may not be isolated. (Note: this Guide only addresses those intermediates produced after the point that the company has defined as the point at which the production of the API begins.)

Lot
See Batch

Lot Number
See Batch Number

Manufacture
All operations of receipt of materials, production, packaging, repackaging, labelling, relabelling, quality control, release, storage, and distribution of APIs and related controls.

Material
A general term used to denote raw materials (starting materials, reagents, solvents), process aids, intermediates, APIs and packaging and labelling materials.

Mother Liquor
The residual liquid which remains after the crystallization or isolation processes. A mother liquor may contain unreacted materials, intermediates, levels of the API and/or impurities. It may be used for further processing.

Packaging Material
Any material intended to protect an intermediate or API during storage and transport.

Procedure
A documented description of the operations to be performed, the precautions to be taken and measures to be applied directly or indirectly related to the manufacture of an intermediate or API.

Process Aids
Materials, excluding solvents, used as an aid in the manufacture of an intermediate or API that do not themselves participate in a chemical or biological reaction (e.g. filter aid, activated carbon, etc).

Process Control
See In-Process Control

Production
All operations involved in the preparation of an API from receipt of materials through processing and packaging of the API.

Qualification
Action of proving and documenting that equipment or ancillary systems are properly installed, work correctly, and actually lead to the expected results. Qualification is part of validation, but the individual qualification steps alone do not constitute process validation.

Quality Assurance (QA)
The sum total of the organised arrangements made with the object of ensuring that all APIs are of the quality required for their intended use and that quality systems are maintained.

Quality Control (QC)
Checking or testing that specifications are met.

Quality Unit(s)
An organizational unit independent of production which fulfills both Quality Assurance and Quality Control responsibilities. This can be in the form of separate QA and QC units or a single individual or group, depending upon the size and structure of the organization.

Quarantine
The status of materials isolated physically or by other effective means pending a decision on their subsequent approval or rejection.

Raw Material
A general term used to denote starting materials, reagents, and solvents intended for use in the production of intermediates or APIs.

Reference Standard, Primary
A substance that has been shown by an extensive set of analytical tests to be authentic material that should be of high purity. This standard can be: (1) obtained from an officially recognised source, or (2) prepared by independent synthesis, or (3) obtained from existing production material of high purity, or (4) prepared by further purification of existing production material.

Reference Standard, Secondary
A substance of established quality and purity, as shown by comparison to a primary reference standard, used as a reference standard for routine laboratory analysis.

Reprocessing
Introducing an intermediate or API, including one that does not conform to standards or specifications, back into the process and repeating a crystallization step or other appropriate chemical or physical manipulation steps (e.g., distillation, filtration, chromatography, milling) that are part of the established manufacturing process. Continuation of a process step after an in-process control test has shown that the step is incomplete is considered to be part of the normal process, and not reprocessing.

Retest Date
The date when a material should be re-examined to ensure that it is still suitable for use.

Reworking
Subjecting an intermediate or API that does not conform to standards or specifications to one or more processing steps that are different from the established manufacturing process to obtain acceptable quality intermediate or API (e.g., recrystallizing with a different solvent).

Signature (signed)
See definition for signed

Signed (signature)
The record of the individual who performed a particular action or review. This record can be initials, full handwritten signature, personal seal, or authenticated and secure electronic signature.

Solvent
An inorganic or organic liquid used as a vehicle for the preparation of solutions or suspensions in the manufacture of an intermediate or API.

Specification
A list of tests, references to analytical procedures, and appropriate acceptance criteria that are numerical limits, ranges, or other criteria for the test described. It establishes the set of criteria to which a material should conform to be considered acceptable for its intended use. "Conformance to specification" means that the material, when tested according to the listed analytical procedures, will meet the listed acceptance criteria.

Validation
A documented program that provides a high degree of assurance that a specific process, method, or system will consistently produce a result meeting pre-determined acceptance criteria.

Validation Protocol
A written plan stating how validation will be conducted and defining acceptance criteria. For example, the protocol for a manufacturing process identifies processing equipment, critical process parameters/operating ranges, product characteristics, sampling, test data to be collected, number of validation runs, and acceptable test results.

Yield, Expected
The quantity of material or the percentage of theoretical yield anticipated at any appropriate phase of production based on previous laboratory, pilot scale, or manufacturing data.

Yield, Theoretical
The quantity that would be produced at any appropriate phase of production, based upon the quantity of material to be used, in the absence of any loss or error in actual production.

Notes

Notes

Notes